MW01205483

Autograph Page

BUILDING WEALTH
From the Ground Up

A Practical & Spiritual Guide to Obtaining Wealth

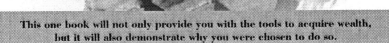

This one book will not only provide you with the tools to acquire wealth,
but it will also demonstrate why you were chosen to do so.

MIKEL BROWN

CJC PUBLISHING COMPANY

EL PASO, TEXAS

Building Wealth from the Ground Up
A Practical & Spiritual Guide to Obtaining Wealth

1208 Sumac Drive
El Paso, TX 79925

Editorial assistance for CJC Publishing Co. by Gary Sparkman

Jacket design by Scott Whittle
Photo by Yolie's Perfection Photography

www.buildinguwealth.com

CONTENTS

Dedication

This book is dedicated to my lovely wife, who has been my inspiration and dream come true. To my children who I love with all my heart...you are my motivation. I cannot forget the many people that have allowed themselves to become my laboratory to develop and test ideas for helping to form their businesses and testing fresh ideas. Keep growing!

Preface

_B__uilding Wealth from the Ground Up_ is a fundamentally sound philosophy on how to gain or regain the wealth that has been lost through one mean or another. I believe that sickness results from stolen health while poverty is the conclusion of stolen wealth. Physical health and financial wealth are two main ingredients necessary for survival in our society that is health conscious and wealth driven. No one can deny the importance of money because it addresses so many aspects of our lives. Money is necessary in order to pay living expenses, doctor and hospital bills, vehicle expenses, family needs, church obligations, and the list goes on. To ignore the necessity of money is to deny the way this world operates. The American free enterprise system is neither fair nor impartial. Our tax procedure rewards the individual who discovers tax loopholes and takes advantage of them, but it punishes the ones who are ignorant of certain tax avoidance strategies that are put in place for those who will examine, scrutinize, and dissect the tax code. Tax attorneys make millions of dollars for helping their corporate and individual clients do just that.

This book is intended to provide a solid, step-by-step system for building your personal wealth and securing your financial future. Herein lies the key to your opportunity to make a substantial amount of money without the thought of ever having to return to your dead-end job. I share in this book the practical and spiritual dimensions of wealth. Financial wealth is not predestined for enjoyment by any small, privileged group of individuals. Rather, anyone can increase his or her prosperity by abandoning a poverty-stricken mentality for a healthier mind set regarding wealth accumulation. This book does not outline any get-rich-quick schemes or high risk, low yield multi-level marketing programs that promise quick returns with little investment of time and money. I will simply help you to identify and apply a few time-tested and proven strategies that will enable you to boost the amount of your income to your desired level. Keep one thing in mind, however. I cannot make you apply any of the principles outlined in this book. As the old adage goes, you can lead a horse to water, but you cannot make him drink.

Wealth exists on the same echelon for those who will invest the time to become a student of the laws that govern wealth and for those who are simply hungry to capture that which has eluded so many Americans. One of the misconceptions about wealth is that you have to be a millionaire in order to claim a wealthy status. Contrary to popular opinion, wealth is not based on how much you make but on how much you get to keep. If, for example, you earn a million dollars a month and $999,999.00 goes out in bills every month, you are simply living a high-priced lifestyle. This indicates that you are no better off than the person who makes only Twenty-five hundred dollars a month with $2,400 going towards bills. Our world is in need of more individuals who will tap its priceless treasures to expose more witty inventions and new concepts for addressing current challenges. I truly believe that there are more than a million ways to create new wealth which have yet to be discovered. Will you be the next Bill Gates, Oprah Winfrey, or New Franchise initiator? Don't let your life, dreams, or vision be flushed down the drain of discouragement. This book will help turn your vision into victory and convert your nightmares into dreams as you discover the dynamics of the **"Building Wealth from the Ground Up."**

1

Gift Wrapped
Wealth

▼

*It is important that you learn how to maximize your
potential for making money, while at the same time
developing your skills to put your money to work for you.*
Mikel Brown

CHAPTER 1

Gift Wrapped Wealth

How often do you find yourself saying: "I wish I knew how to start a business and build wealth?" Do you need to make more money? It's a shame for you not to make more money when some people do it so easily. My aim is to dispel the myths about wealth and reveal a few special tips to help keep your fears from holding YOU back and to get you started on the path to developing your business and building wealth, now! If you are serious about wanting to start your business and build wealth, use these nuggets on how to make more money, and to make your money work for you! Guaranteed! These special tips helped me make more money and I am certain that they will work for YOU too.

Wealth Distribution Statistics by the United Nations revealed a staggering reality of wealth distribution in 1999. The United Nations Development Program (UNDP) reported in 1998 that the world's 225 richest people now have a combined wealth of $1 trillion. That's equal to the combined annual income of the world's 2.5 billion poorest people. As of 1995 (the latest figures available), Federal Reserve research found that the wealth of the top one percent of Americans is greater than that of the bottom 95 percent. Three years earlier, the Fed's Survey of Consumer Finance found that the top one percent had wealth greater than the bottom 90 percent.

Why would you suggest such a disparity in wealth? What is the top one percent of America's richest doing that the bottom 95 percent have not yet caught on to? Is the top one percent richest in America more intelligent than the lower populace? Is it true that the rich are

> *What you don't know can choke the life out of you.*

getting richer and the poor is getting poorer? Allow me to propose that one of America's middle to lower income family bracket's greatest problems is a low IQ concerning finances. What you don't know can choke the life out of you. It is important that you learn how to maximize your potential for making money, while at the same time developing your skills to put your money to work for you. African Americans and Hispanics are the least informed ethnic groups in America on financial matters. The modest net worth of white families is 8 times that of African-Americans and 12 times that of Hispanics. The median financial wealth of African-Americans (net worth less home equity) is $200 (one percent of the $18,000 for whites) while that of Hispanics is zero. Microsoft CEO Bill Gates has more wealth than the bottom 45 percent of American households combined. The problem is that most African Americans and Hispanics have not unraveled the package of their potential to create wealth.

Stock market participation is broad but remarkably shallow. Although more American adults own stocks and stock mutual funds than at any time in history, 71 percent of households own no shares at all or hold less than $2,000, including mutual funds and popular 401(k) plans. Don't allow financial jargon to discourage you from investigating further into the matter of investing. You can increase the money you made quicker by using investment vehicles that can potentially increase your net worth exponentially. Most non-investors get turned off to this financial terminology which is inundated with numbers and acronyms. Let's face it, it can be overwhelming and cause you to feel ignorant. Rests assure; help is on the way. There are books and periodicals in your local bookstores that can make you an informed investor and bring you up to speed on the subject of finances. Investments are just one of the ways you can increase your wealth, but it's not the only way.

> ## Money cannot produce increase if you are afraid to use it.

Imagine receiving a package with a nice colorful wrapping paper and a pretty little gold bow tied on top of the package. Your immediate response is "Wow! I wonder what's inside." Your speculation of the gift-wrapped package is unwarranted because you are now the proud owner of the package. All there is left for you to do in order to alleviate the suspense is open the package. You are that package waiting to be opened. But in order to unlock the treasures stored inside, you must be willing to do it yourself. It sounds easier than it actually is. Most people avoid responsibility because they refuse to accept it on the premise that they are too afraid to make mistakes. Making mistakes are a part of life, and it will remain that way until the end of the world. So don't sweat the small things. Money cannot produce increase if you are afraid to use it.

Contentment is the lid for conclusion and the route towards procrastination. When it comes to success, remember that its process is a journey not a destination. Contentment is not the completion of your potential; it is only a marker to indicate satisfaction. One of the things that I respect about Donald Trump is his desire to continue to reach for what others claim that he has enough of. He is the top real estate developer in New York. But that was not always the case. In 1991 Donald Trump was nine hundred million in the red. It may not have been so bad if he had only owed zero (broke even), but he owed nine hundred million dollars. Donald Trump displayed great courage, with a never die attitude, and climbed back passed his critics up to the top to become New York's greatest real estate developers. The principle that Donald Trump applied can work on any economic level. Today, Donald Trump's net worth is approximately Five Billion dollars. That's not bad considering just a little over a decade ago he was broke. Adjusting for inflation, the net worth of the median American household fell 10 percent between 1989 and 1997, declining from $54,600 to $49,900. The net worth of the top one percent is now 2.4 times the combined wealth of the poorest 80 percent. Jesus made a statement of truth and said, "The poor you will have with you always..." He was not saying that some people are destined for poverty. But what others may not have understood what Jesus alluded to was the fact that there will always be people that are unwilling to do what is necessary in order to get

> *Contentment is not the completion of your potential; it is only a marker to indicate satisfaction.*

ahead. However, poverty is not what a person is; poverty is how a person thinks.

Your wealth is gift wrapped in a beautiful human package which goes by the name (put your name here). You are your greatest asset! How much money you accumulate in your life time has not yet been determined! Consider your mind, your hands, and your body. They are all tools used in this society to make money. Some people get paid for thinking, some people receive compensation

> **Creating wealth is not a privilege; it is an inalienable right.**

for working with their hands, and some even get paid by using their body. Creating wealth is not a privilege; it is an inalienable right. It cannot be argued legitimately under any circumstances. The heart beating in your chest, points to the existence of a real-live human being, which substantiates a persons rights to manufacture money and wealth. The one thing that being alive doesn't do is guarantees one's success. That, my friend, depends solely on the choice of the individual.

Every human being performs on the grand stage of planet earth. Jack Nicholson, James Brown, Paul McCartney, Michael Jackson, Halle Berry, Denzel Washington, Bill Gates, Tiger Woods, Steven Spielberg, Oprah Winfrey, Ministers, Store Managers and Clerks, CEOs, Secretaries, Teachers, Law Enforcement Officers and many more occupations are all exchanging the use of their mental and physical faculties for some dollar amount. Recognize your gift; develop and train it to produce lasting wealth!

Taking the Braces Off of Your Legs

▼

People cripple themselves with unwarranted excuses.
Mikel Brown

CHAPTER 2

Taking the Braces Off of Your Legs

I can recall the 1994 movie titled Forrest Gump, starring Tom Hanks as Forrest Gump. In the movie, Forrest was often teased and bullied at school by the other boys because he had a certain learning handicap that caused him to process information much slower than the other kids and he also had a physical handicap of the legs. Young Forrest was oftentimes teased because of the leg braces he had to wear as a result of under-developed leg muscles. On one particular day, however, something very unusual happened as a few of the boys began to chase Forrest while on their bikes. In his endeavor to flee their intended brutality, Forrest, hindered at first by the bulky leg braces, gathered so much momentum in his efforts to flee that he ran right out of the braces, leaving behind his little female friend who could only yell, "Run Forrest! Run!" And boy did he run. The point here is that Forrest Gump, when under fire, responded to the challenge by stretching his legs with strides that the braces could no longer restrict. Consequently, the braces broke loose and fell off, leaving Forrest Gump to run free for the very first time in his life. And once freed, he never again looked back to the one handicap that had once restricted his mobility.

Many people have some impediment operating in their lives that restricts them from reaching new heights. Although certain traumatic experiences of the past may be long gone, what remains in many cases are handicaps that we impose on ourselves. In affect, we choose to wear braces that have outlived their usefulness. As creatures of habit, we can become so accustomed to operating with self-imposed restraints that we come to believe we are unable to function without them. As a result, many people decide to avoid those stress-producing situations that serve to measure the quality of their recovery. The avoidance stems from a fear of having to possibly face the pain felt during the initial injury. When people choose instead to face the difficult challenges that threaten their future, they will discover that the very objects that restrict mobility will fall off as they exercise their need to achieve. When this happens, they will find that they have the ability to run far and fast.

> *You can either articulate what you see or you can communicate what you want to see.*

He who is good for making excuses is seldom good for anything else. People cripple themselves with unwarranted excuses. In fact, many of their excuses are given without them ever attempting anything.. Your success in life, business or marriage, is primarily based on your ability to harness your tongue by refusing to voice your frustrations. One of the most difficult challenges you will ever face is controlling your speech. The tongue has destroyed more businesses, dreams, ministries, and marriages than any device known to man. For the ability to construct a bright or gloomy existence resides within the power of our words. We must be mindful to ensure that we utter the kind of speech that will create the atmosphere most conducive to the success desired. I look at it this way; you can either articulate what you see or you can communicate what you want to see. Since you do it all the time, why not deliberately express what you want to see!

> *Feeling good about yourself is not a matter of what happens to you, but a matter of you controlling what you want to happen.*

Feeling good about yourself is not a matter of what happens to you, but a matter of you controlling what you want to happen. To say that you have a low self-esteem based on the negative things that may have occurred in your life simply perpetuates feelings of self-doubt that over time can lead to depression. I wonder what your life would be like if you had chosen to defeat the thing that made you capitulate your dream. How strong and confident would you be today if you did not drop out of college but went on to receive your degree?

Where would you be if you had not gotten pregnant out of wedlock and, as a result, not stopped pursuing your goals? How much closer to your dream would you be if you had not joined the military when you did or taken that factory job in order to meet an immediate need? What would you be doing now? This question is very important so listen closely. How much money would you be making now if you had taken that leadership role offered to you some years ago? Do a self examination and see if you have restrictions placed on you that have hindered your prospects for a prosperous future.

There are two kinds of paralysis that can affect people. One is considered physical and the other is mental. For the moment, I would like to focus on those individuals who suffer from paralysis of the mind because it is these individuals who do not pursue their dreams for fear of the unknown. No one can make you inferior without your consent. One person can

> **Excuses are the voice of discouragement, pessimism and depression.**

have no arms and hands while another person can have the complete use of all their faculties and still be unsuccessful. Take for instance, Joni, a paraplegic who can neither walk nor use her arms. Despite her condition, she draws and paints better than most people who enjoy the full use of their arms and hands. Joni defies her handicap by using her mouth to hold the paintbrush in order to draw and paint. Most people fail to accomplish their goals in life because they are more concerned with what they do not have than what they possess. The frustrated many who have settled for living well below their personal desires will usually offer many excuses for why they have fallen short of their financial objectives in life. And at the top of the list you can find excuses such as the lack of money, support, contacts, education, and wrong skin color.

The fear that prevents people from pursuing their dreams of success can be appropriately classified as self-imposed mental paralysis. Such fear is induced whenever we experience the pressure of having to make decisions we feel we are not ready to make or start journeys we feel we are not ready to begin. As a kid, my mother never allowed me to make excuses whenever I felt too afraid to face my academic challenges. Whenever I would offer reasons why I could not attend school on a certain test day, I can vividly recall my mother simply telling me, "Don't give me that lame excuse!" in addition to a few other choice words. Excuses are dream killers, and they eat away at your confidence and certainty. Excuses are the voice of discouragement, pessimism and depression. They have the potential to render you more crippled and helpless than blindness or paraplegia. Remember! If you can avoid articulating your excuses, your opposition will have no voice. You can dig your grave or build your palace with your mouth. What you can do and what you cannot do derives from the same place—your mouth. If you can control your mouth, ninety percent of your goals are attainable.

> *You can dig your grave or build your palace with your mouth.*

To believe something is one thing, but to conceive it is another. The power to produce a thing is ever present within you, but the seed to germinate that very thing is not always readily at hand. Your greatest potential lies within you as an untapped precious mineral, simply waiting for a motivational message powerful enough to break through to that dormant area where your greatest aspirations lie. It is in that sacred place of the soul where encouraging words give dreams their life. Just as pregnancy cannot happen unless the male seed enters the vaginal canal to fertilize the female egg, so too must a motivating word in seed form enter the heart of every dreamer in order to give life to a dream. It is the power of the life-giving word that starts the growing process of your vision. Understand that there are no spiritual wombs that cannot produce, but the exception to this rule does exist for those who reject the seed.

What is in me that I cannot perform on my own? What potential lies deep within the belly of my spirit and in the crevasses of my thoughts? What do I need to do in order to insert life into my dreams or vision? Loneliness is not a loss of affection, but a loss of direction. If you are sitting at home hoping someone will come and change your life, your seat may tire of carrying the load of your dead weight. There comes a time when your failures will kiss destiny and destiny will beg to be fulfilled. You cannot hide behind your past failures or your insecurities forever.

> *You have more working for you than against you.*

We are quick to accept our individual failures as the documentation that guarantees our future failure. Truth be told, people often focus more on their deficiencies than their internal treasures. You have more working for you than against you. Take off your mental brace and you will discover that you can do more without it.

$$3$$

Jewish Secrets
to Wealth

*Each Successful Jew has an obligation to help
support another Jew in business.*
Mikel Brown

CHAPTER 3

Jewish Secrets to Wealth

My purpose for writing this chapter stems not from any prejudice or bias concerning Jewish people. Rather, I desire to offer here some very powerful insights into the mystery of why the Jews as a whole are a very wealthy group of people. Just as African Americans had to endure a very dark chapter in American history, Jews have a legacy of suffering that dates all the way back to their conception as a people. And through it all, they have found the wherewithal to persevere and prosper under the most adverse conditions. Hitler's name is synonymous with evil and evokes much speculation as to whether he was the antichrist because of the genocidal atrocities he committed against the Jewish people. I have a great deal of respect for the Jewish people and their culture, and I believe that they can offer us a wealth of understanding regarding the subject of money.

Jews rank as the riches ethnic group in the world followed by the Chinese. Within these two groups exists a certain mind set regarding economic empowerment both within their national borders and abroad. But what is interesting is that the most populace group, the Chinese, on the planet ranks second to the least populace group, the Jews, in terms of worldwide economic clout. How can this be? What accounts for why one of the smallest nations of people has prospered in every corner of the earth and has done so for so many years? What is the secret to why Jewish people enjoy so much prosperity in a world that is so blatantly prejudiced against them?

Predominant throughout large cities like New York, Chicago, and Los Angeles is their stamp of ownership as Jewish names can be read on prestigious law firms, department stores, advertising agencies, banks, hospitals, and major real estate properties. Furthermore, a stroll through many small rural towns will also reveal Jewish names on many of the local grocery and hardware stores, doctors' offices, medical clinics, and gas stations, indicating again Jewish ownership. Is this reality a coincidence or is it the result of a deliberate effort on the part of Jewish people? While most Americans teach their children how not to be poor, Jews teach their children how to prosper instead. There is a vast difference in the methodologies of the two philosophical approaches to building wealth.

The majority of the problems that Americans face regarding wealth building and money management may have more to do with the system of formal education in America than anything else. As our children matriculate through the education system, they soon learn which occupations in our society offer the highest compensation for their talents. Thus they begin mapping out their career choices at very earlier ages to secure the largest possible wage commensurate with their academic achievement. The flaw in such a system is that it does not teach our young adults how to make millions or become self-employed business owners. Instead, it teaches them how to qualify for a job with reliable insurance benefits and a good pension plan. Consequently, most Americans are wage earners who are struggling with mountains of debt and many are just waiting for that day when they can settle into their retirement years. While many individuals have begun steering their children in the direction of professional athletics, corporate management, or the Armed Services to secure their financial futures, Jewish parents encourage their children to own professional sports teams as well as major corporations. And if not owners, then they become major stockholders in corporations.

How do Jewish people make their money? How do many Jewish businessmen borrow money without going through a bank? Why are there so many millionaires of Jewish decent? What is the secret for why they consistently out-perform Western businessmen? These questions are vital to understanding not only the why, but the how-to as well. Inquiring minds would like to know the answers to the aforementioned questions. I have never seen a Jewish synagogue positioned along a row of storefront business establishments; nor have I ever seen a synagogue in a state of dilapidation. Jewish people take special pride in worshiping their God in the best facilities their monies can buy. They refuse to believe that just any building can accommodate their worship. The more the Jewish community prospers, the more it invests in its synagogues. The more investment of wealth into their synagogues, the more God will bless them, as is their belief. Their outlook on taking care of what, to them, is the most important aspect of community may account for why the Jewish community prospers so abundantly.

The Jewish view of economy is unlike that of any other group of people on the face of the earth. They are taught from early childhood to care for and help their Jewish brothers and sisters succeed in all facets of life. I suppose that as a result of their long history of being an oppressed people, they have developed an innate tendency toward building strong communities by their generous investments on both corporate and individual levels. When it comes to furthering the cause of Jewish businesses and individuals, money is never the object to stand in the way of their achievement. This strong sense of community is absolutely foreign to most of the other ethnic groups in the United States such as African Americans, Latinos, American Indians, and Caucasians. Where most people embrace the practice of getting ahead at the expense of others, Jews will stick together in order to get ahead.

> **The importance of a healthy self-esteem is not a debatable issue among the Jewish people.**

Each successful Jew has an obligation to help support another Jew in business. They commit to doing business with their own people before doing business with any other race. As a result, they succeed by maintaining the basic principle of looking out for the welfare of their communities.

Imagine the financial possibilities of being able to promote your business within a network of national and international businesses where every bid proposal you submitted to the group received priority consideration. Were this the case, your business would be assured phenomenal financial success. This practice, in effect, is the secret for why the success rate amongst Jewish business ventures is higher than for any other ethnic group on earth. Their propensity to give deferential consideration to each other in business ensures that the monies earned from the sale of their goods and services to everyone else remain in the family. Is this practice wrong? Not at all! Jewish businessmen understand the importance of first investing their resources within their close-knit networks before allowing their financial capital to leave the community.

Interwoven throughout the economic and social fabric of Jewish culture is a solid understanding and consistent application of certain Old Testament biblical principles of financial stewardship. Judaism teaches its adherents to give a tenth of their income to the local synagogue to ensure its upkeep and provide for the financial needs of those individuals who labor in various capacities within the ministry. According to Old Testament Jewish practice, businessmen involved in agricultural husbandry were required to provide for the poor by allowing them to glean the crops at the corners of their fields. The land owners could neither harvest the corners of their fields for personal or business use nor pass over their fields a second time to gather any crops missed in the first gleaning. This was, in a sense, the Jewish form of social welfare and God's method of caring for the needs of the poor. Those who would follow this basic rule of providing for the less fortunate would ensure that even the poor would be privileged to eat at the expense of the wealthy landowners. This practice is foreign to American businessmen. As a result, the poor in most countries around the world must depend on government agencies for support. This form of welfare serves only to cripple a people while placing an undue burden on society.

It is important to note that Jewish people define success

much differently than do typical Americans. The Hebrew word for "prosper" suggests that which flourishes or succeeds. This word occurs some 65 times in the text of the Hebrew Old Testament. It generally connotes the idea of a successful venture, and is sometimes used in such a way as to indicate "victory." Jews place a higher premium on the journey to achieve success than on its actual obtainment. Jewish children are taught that the many stairs one has to climb to obtain success is more important than where he or she may rank on the ladder of success. Their philosophical approach to the overall issue of financial achievement stems from the importance they attach to self-esteem.

> *Jewish people believe that wealth is an entitlement of birthright and not of achievement.*

The importance of a healthy self-esteem is not a debatable issue among the Jewish people. It is placed at the top of their hierarchy of needs and sets the azimuth for all their pursuits in life. Jewish children learn at an early age that their value and worth to society derives from the priceless, intrinsic talents and abilities inherited at birth and not from the fruit of one's accomplishments. Judaism starts from the premise that each human being is created in the image of God. From this awareness, problems with self-worth are seldom the big issue among Jews as among other ethnic groups. The Western mind set appraises the value of self much differently. In Western cultures, the barometer of self-esteem is lowered or raised based upon certain external, superficial, transitory trappings of success such as education, income level, occupation, private club memberships, or size of home owned. While most Americans gain their self-respect from these things, Jewish people view them merely as the blessings that result from the careful cultivation of those treasures resident within every person. In essence, Jews are taught not to make the mistake of attaching self-worth to social status.

While many people derive their understanding of self from Charles Darwin's flawed theory of evolution, adherents of Judaism gain their self-awareness from ancient scriptures that reveal man's origin in the creative works of God. Rather than being merely a higher form of animal on Darwin's scale of evolution, creationist believe that God created man in His own image. And it is this image of self that Jewish children are taught to embrace. Jewish people believe that wealth is an entitlement of birthright and not of achievement. Jews who follow closely the teachings of their faith believe that God created them and placed in them His nature, One that knows only success. They understand that when they simply exist as who they were born to be, the evidence of success will eventually flow into their lives.

In our society, money is the one commodity without equal. For most Americans, it determines how we keep score. The general consensus in this nation is that we don't have enough of it. I emphatically disagree! I say that we don't know what to do with the money we have. Money has the potential of bringing out the best or the worst in people. The best way to ruin a man who doesn't know how to handle money is by giving him some of it. How people manage their financial affairs reveals much about their character. The methods they employ to earn it and the areas they choose to spend it speak volumes about certain of their internal motivations. Although money cannot solve the majority of life's most perplexing problems, it can, however, address those problems that develop from the lack of it.

John D. Rockefeller is quoted as saying, "*I believe the power to make money is a gift from God.*" The bible is very clear on the issue of how God regards the prosperity of his people. In the eighth chapter of Deuteronomy in the Bible, the great law-giver, Moses, admonishes the Jewish people not to forget that it is God who blesses His people to acquire wealth. From this, it is clear that the power to obtain wealth is a gift that God alone gives to mankind. And without question, staunch adherents of Judaism

> *The best way to ruin a man who doesn't know how to handle money is by giving him some of it.*

truly believe that, as children of God, they are blessed with the strength and ability to prosper because of an Old Testament covenant that they continue to enjoy to this very day.

The ability to reach great heights does not depend upon our natural talents and abilities. Jews believe that the effort involved in the pursuit of achieving greatness is man's responsibility, but the results are strictly left to God to multiply and increase. In effect, God will provide what we need to succeed while we have put forth the effort to achieve the success that He has promised to His people. The key to living a prosperous and fulfilling life is that you find something you love to do and you'll never have to work hard a day in your life.

Although Jewish people have a very remarkable propensity for making money and accumulating wealth, it must never be forgotten that they are as equally inclined to donate large sums of money to very worthy causes. Jews are unmatched in the area of philanthropy. They live by the "Golden Rule" principle that you do unto others as you would have others to do unto you. They are very mindful of the fact that they have a civic obligation to give back to the same communities a portion of the prosperity that makes their enriched lives possible. The example set by Jews in the area of financial management should resonate strongly with any people desiring to improve their financial plight, for it is an example of a people who, against great odds, have been able to amass substantial wealth for the Jewish community.

4

Practical Wealth

▼

The road to wealth should be a
well-planned, methodical journey
Mikel Brown

| CHAPTER 4 |

Practical Wealth

T he road to wealth should be a well-planned, methodical journey. Building a solid financial foundation requires both skillful planning and time. Anyone seeking to secure his or her financial future must ensure that diversification across a broad array of business markets is a crucial part of the investment strategy. In my book "Beyond Ordinary: Success is Only a Thought Away" I discussed one of the techniques for accumulating wealth by throwing some of the money you make today into your tomorrow by placing portions of it in any number of investment vehicles. You may choose to invest small amounts of your income in an annuity, mutual funds, stocks and bonds, certificates of deposit, IRA's, and or a 401K plan. If you follow your plan consistently over a period of time, you will be amazed at how quickly your money will grow. The point is that you must utilize time to your advantage by implementing a well thought out investment plan immediately.

As we march toward our golden years, nothing can bring a greater sense of peace to the soul than knowing that in our

---

youth we were wise enough to cast some of today's money into our tomorrow. It's a good feeling just knowing that, in your retirement years, your standard of living will not be left to chance. And it's an even better feeling to be in control of how and when you get to that momentous day of retirement.

Many individuals who have wisely invested for their future look forward to the day when they can finally retire. Yet the closer they get, the more they wonder how they are going to manage their money so that it will last from that point on. There are many different types of investment vehicles available to investors that would enable them to fund their retirements. If chosen wisely, these plans can

> *A financial planner can help you make decisions that will enable you to make the most of your financial resources.*

provide multiple income streams that will more than replace most incomes. But is retirement your main interest now or is building wealth your primary concern. If you are under forty years of age, you are perhaps helplessly in love with living life to its fullest. If you are over the age of forty, then I am certain that you have already begun to take life more seriously as you are now more aware that time is of the essence.

In the early eighties I sold insurance and investments. Oftentimes I would help my clients by performing a financial needs and risk analysis to show them in black and white where they were in terms of their insurance coverage and assets. Once the analysis was completed, I would then outline the steps that they needed to take in order to achieve their financial objectives. Financial planning is the process of wisely managing your finances so that you can achieve your dreams and goals while at the same time helping you negotiate the financial barriers that inevitably arise in every stage of life. Managing your personal finances is ultimately your responsibility. However, you don't have to do it alone. A financial planner can help you make decisions that will enable you to make the most of your financial resources.

> *You can earn more money on your IRA by paying as early as possible in the year.*

Since I have been taking flying lessons, I have been able to use my flying experience to draw analogies between flying and financial planning. Financial Planners are like the Cessna planes in which many inexperienced flyers must take their lessons. The Cessna 150 is designed to make flying easy. If, while flying, a pilot ever has the unfortunate encounter of experiencing vertigo, the trained response is to let go of the controls and allow the plane to correct itself. The problem, however, is that some pilots cannot find it within themselves to trust the plane's instrument panel. When a Cessna plane crashes, it is more often than not the result of the pilot's unwillingness to release the controls and trust the instrumentation. Financial planners are like the instrument panels of the Cessna. As the pilot of your own destiny, you must trust that a good financial planner can help stir you to your financial destination if you would adhere to their advice.

With corporate fraud and scandal so pervasive in our society, confidence in the integrity of corporate managers has every investor asking whether their funds are safe in the hands of corporate officers. Should people go back to putting their money under their mattresses or hiding it in their pillowcases? You really have no reason to worry about losing your investments with fund companies if they should file bankruptcy. As a fund investor, you are protected from such fund-company disasters by the Investment Company Act of 1940. Under the act, each fund is set up as an individual company, separate from the fund sponsor and owned only by its shareholders. In essence, your

> *Sell any of your under-performing mutual funds in order to acquire better performing ones.*

fund hires the fund company to manage its assets. Even if the fund-company were to file bankruptcy, creditors would not be able to touch any of the money invested in that company.

When it comes to IRA's (Individual Retirement Account), most people look to only apply their $2000 close to the end of the year for tax purposes. By delaying the investment of money to the end of the year, they are losing out on earning accrued interest. You can earn more money on your IRA by paying as early as possible in the year. Plus, it will give your money the benefit of tax-free accumulation for as long as possible. Over time this strategy will make all the difference in the world. Anyone can build wealth through investing. You don't need a lot of money to make a lot of money. All you need is the prudence in how to invest your money and be willing to leave it for at least five to ten years. The economy will fluctuate, but learn to be patient.

I do not claim to be an expert in all money matters, but I do know something when money matters. Allow me to offer one quick note that I believe will help the average person who may not have millions in the bank or whose net worth may be currently in the basement. Do not judge yourself and sentence your future to where you are in life at this moment. With faith in God, and determination and fortitude in your heart, your future can be brighter than ever before. Go ahead and make your first million. I believe you can do it!

> **There often exists a tremendous opportunity to reap huge dividends by choosing to invest in the very stocks that everyone else is clamoring to unload.**

From these lessons, we are able to learn a great deal about how the rich and famous invest their money. Peeking inside the investment world of the wealthy is as compelling as reading about their professional accomplishments. There are many shrewd celebrities who have access to some of the best investment advise by some of the country's top financial advisors. The latest investment secret floating around is that people should capitalize on the potential by purchasing stock in unpleasant news. I know that this advice can probably cause some serious investors to be repulsed, but sometimes making your investment choices based on bad news can work in your favor. There often exists a tremendous opportunity to reap huge dividends by choosing to invest in the very stocks that everyone else is clamoring to unload.

In the mid nineties, Microsoft announced that it was no longer considering the acquisition of Intuit, the maker of

Quicken financial planning software. This news caused Intuit's stock to plummet more than twelve dollars in one day. The fortunate thing was that the stock quickly recovered and people who bought stock during this time were able to benefit from bad news. Here is a wonderful strategy for selling. If a stock's price falls 10% from the price you paid for it, sell it. I heard one investor say that a typical market cycle lasts three years, which should be enough time to consider whether to sell or hold onto your mutual funds. Sell any of your under-performing mutual funds in order to acquire better performing ones. You can make anything work, if you learn how to work it.

How to Control Your Flow of Income

▼

*Your challenge will appear when
your prior knowledge begins to
clash with your new knowledge.*
Mikel Brown

---|CHAPTER 5|---

How to Control Your Flow of Income

F or many years, people have relied on the principle of investing for the purpose of getting a return without regard for balancing their faith with works. It is important that people be taught how to apply the basic, practical approaches to investing instead of those unproven methods that claim to return out-of-this-world results. I truly believe that the flow of income can come from both natural and supernatural means. When the door to your account is open, things can flow in and out. In most cases the outgo will determine the income. In either case, you can control the natural as well as the supernatural. Your challenge will appear when your prior knowledge begins to clash with your new knowledge. Fear and doubt will attempt to infiltrate your pattern of thought in order to render you immobile and ineffective.

In general, life itself is business! Regardless of how you look at it, life boils down to being one huge negotiation. A baby negotiates for milk or attention by crying; a toddler cooperates with the parent for a piece of candy; a teenager compromises for the use of the family vehicle; and adults negotiate in marriage and in business for wage increases, etc. I think you understand the point I am making here. If a person does not have a basic understanding of how income is derived, then surely they will not understand the principle of electromagnetism. I don't want you to think for one minute that this is a lesson on science. Rather, I wish to point out that you and I are the magnets that will attract wealth. Science allows man to understand those universal laws that govern our lives through the scientific method of arranging facts and information in a manner that exposes truth. My purpose here is to inform and not to bore you. Therefore, in order to bring the point home, let me share a powerful one-line statement of truth. Income (what comes in) can only be determined by what goes out!

You may be asking yourselves, what does all this science jargon has to do with the subject at hand. I am merely using certain science related terminology to draw an analogy. My aim is to show how you can improve your financial situation. The key to understanding your present financial condition is based on knowing what went out yesterday. It is always very easy to identify a person who does not understand why he or she is in a certain financial condition. "How," you may be asking yourself. The answer lies in the fact that they question the amount of their income.

> *What comes in today will always reflect what went out yesterday.*

What comes in today will always reflect what went out yesterday. If I want my income to increase, I have to put out something that will substantiate increase. A person cannot just sit back, do nothing, and expect his or her income to increase magically.

Electromagnetism affects everything in our universe. The laws of attraction and repulsion operate by means of electromagnet waves that cause like objects to be attracted to other like objects. I can always guess, with a great deal of certainty, the level of a person's income by simply knowing the income of their ten closest friends. Your income will usually fall somewhere within the average income range of your ten closest friends. If you want your income to increase, you don't have to get rid of your closest friends; simply shuffle them around.

With the right material leaving your hand, you can build your heaven on earth. Your thoughts are the forerunners of every change that occurs in your life. You are responsible for activating every emotion in your life. You have already predetermined what and how a situation will affect you. Consequently, only you can determine the flow of your income. The conscious mind is the portion of the mind we use to establish our goals and dreams. The conscious mind allows us to become goal-setters. It enables man to establish plans and set goals. On the other hand, the subconscious mind is susceptible to suggestion and is capable of deductive reasoning. The subconscious mind performs best when the conscious mind is in a condition of suspended activity. The subconscious mind is the goal-getter; it develops the power and strength to get the job done.

> *With the right material leaving your hand, you can build your heaven on earth.*

You must first believe that your income can increase and that it will not happen simply as the result of luck or chance. Understand that it is only due to a deliberate action on your part that financial increase will occur. Belief is based on the existence of an accepted thought. Whatever consumes your mind determines where you live. For example, you can live in a mansion, but you can change the reality of your condition by regarding your house as a dump. Remember! It is your outlook on life that determines whether your glass will be either half full or half empty.

A man's life is what his thoughts make it. The creative potential of the human mind is simply astounding. And because we think in pictures, we possess the most powerful tool available for constructing the image of how we desire our lives to be.

> *A man's life is what his thoughts make it.*

Creative imagination will allow you to attract the kind of success you long to enjoy. Before words and symbols can have any real meaning to us, our minds must convert them into pictures that we can understand. People will never change until they have a mental photograph of themselves in their changed position. What you picture or imagine, you will become. Napoleon is reported to have said, "Imagination rules the world."

The Practical Side to Income

The practical approach to controlling the flow of your income is as simple as 1, 2, 3, but its implementation demands discipline. Being rich is not the same as being wealthy. How does a rich person differ from a wealthy individual? A rich person is one who is just as consumed with spending money as he is with making it. This individual is more focused on what money can buy than how it performs. On the other hand, a wealthy person is not so eager to spend the money he labored so hard to earn. The wealthy are like farmers who plant seeds in their fields. With earnest expectation, they wait patiently for that time when they can harvest and enjoy the returns. Wealthy folk enjoy watching their money work hard in the economy. To them, watching their money perform outweighs any thrill that can be felt by spending it.

> *It is easier to make money than to keep it.*

It is easier to make money than to keep it. Building a great financial empire is a difficult task to accomplish. In this country, mighty empires have been lost because they fell into the hands of people who did not appreciate the precious sacrifice required to build them. First generation wealthy individuals understand the price that must be paid to establish financial legacies because their sweat and tears have made it possible. Subsequent generations may not regard what is handed down to them with the same degree of respect.

Today, people are able to create financial empires literally over night. Certain industries make this possible. Consider how quickly certain television and movie stars, musicians, and professional athletes are able to earn millions. Because of how quickly money is made nowadays, most people in the movie industry and athletes demonstrate little respect for the money they make. Their sole interest seems to be stockpiling huge amounts of "bling-bling" all for the sake of image. Many of them choose to live life without an investment plan for the riches they are able to produce. As a result, you can read tabloid tales of many prominent celebrities having to file bankruptcy because they chose to live beyond their means. This kind of ridiculous spending that leads to ruin is tantamount to foolishness.

I believe that every penny earned represents an opportunity to create a vast financial empire, depending on how one chooses to invest what comes into his possession. The way that I view the precious resources that flow into my life differs from the perspective most people hold. For instance, I do not make it a practice of carrying cash in my pocket because of the propensity I have to spend the money on me without regarding how fast it goes. Recently, I needed a few dollars to pay for a haircut, but I did not want to use my credit card at an ATM and be charged $2.00 to get the cash needed. Not only would I have paid the $2.00 ATM fee, but my bank would have also charged me an additional $1.50 to $3.00 for using an ATM machine belonging to another financial institution. Consequently, I went to a local grocery store and purchased something I could eat and enjoy and then got an additional amount without being assessed additional fees. Did I have to do it this way? Am I some cheapskate always looking to save a dollar? No, I'm not. I could have paid the fees and not been affected at all by the charge debited from my account. The ability to use my money wisely is the principle. I can either use it to make the bank richer at my expense or I can use it to accumulate more money to invest. A dollar saved is a value; a dollar invested is increase.

> **A dollar saved is a value; a dollar invested is increased.**

You must learn to control that which is controllable. You and I cannot control whether the stocks and bonds we buy today will outperform the rest of the market tomorrow. There are no guarantees with investments, but there is calculated risk involved. If I can intelligently analyze the performance of management in a company, I can minimize my risks. I believe in investing in the person who is running the company because a company is only as good as the one in charge. There are other factors that I can control such as brokerage and agent fees and ownership costs (excessive annual expenses). By doing this, I can ensure that my future can be bright and that my retirement years are my better years.

Controlling Your Waste

A person once asked me a question while attending one of my Kingdom Management Seminars. The question was with regard to the condition of someone who had a modest income and very little disposable income remaining after paying their bills. The person basically wanted to know how someone in such a predicament could get ahead in life. If you are a person who does not have a lot of money left over after paying your bills, there is a wonderful solution that I would offer in order for anyone with limited financial means to increase his or her income with the money one already has. Most people who claim to have no money are usually people who waste it.

> *Most people who claim to have no money are usually people who waste it.*

Isn't it funny that people who say that they have no money can usually find it for what they really want? Money never truly dissipates; it just moves from one place to the next place. In my Kingdom Management Seminars, I teach on "Controlling Your Waste." I can remember, in one of my seminars conducted, the look on the faces of the seminar attendees when I gave the topic. It was a look of bewilderment and incomprehension. People waste money all the time. Controlling your waste is something I discovered in desperation. If we are cognizant of our waste and where it is place, we can then consciously control our insignificant leftovers and redirect it for better use.

> *Money never truly dissipates; it just moves from one place to the next place.*

Do you oftentimes go to the store and purchase odds and ends? If you use cash, what do you do with your leftover change? Some people put it in the ashtray in their vehicle. Others leave loose cash in their clothes pocket. Yet, some buy quarter bubble gum for their children. So, what do you do with it? Do you save it so that you can give the exact amount to the cashier? I started saving my loose change some fifteen years ago and, to say the least, I have accumulated thousands with what I have invested. Some of it was invested into the lives of people, the church, and various financial accounts. When I buy something with cash, I deliberately make sure that I don't give the exact amount so that I can get the loose change to control. I seldom ever spend money without the intent of wisely redirecting the leftovers. If people will change how they see their leftover change and take a different approach to its use, it will indeed increase their wealth, although not overnight. Wouldn't it be wonderful to never again say that you do not have any money left? By controlling your waste you will find that you will have enough change to invest in mutual funds every month. You can invest as little as $25 a month with some mutual fund plans. Take advantage of what you do have by not considering your leftovers as waste. If you have change, you have more than the person who claims to have nothing.

Breaking the Mentality of "Just Enough"

▼

No danger can arise in rooting out bad principles.
Mikel Brown

| CHAPTER 6 |

Breaking the Mentality
of "Just Enough"

Allow me to explain the word mentality. First of all it is a way of thinking, a philosophy, tendency or a compulsion. A compulsion suggests the existence of a force that causes a thing to be channeled in a certain direction. Although you may want to change a certain pattern of behavior in your life, some unidentified force continues to cause you to go in the same direction. Because most people fail to recognize certain undesirable behavior patterns affecting their choices in life, they continue to experience the recurring problems that relegate them to the same predicament. Although a person may experience temporary relief at times, they will inevitably find themselves in familiar surroundings.

The root of anything reveals both the essence and source of life for that very thing. In order to eliminate the problematic issues that we face in life, we must first deal with the root of our problems. For unless we address the root cause of any undesired condition, we will continue to see the same problems return. Over the years, we develop many bad

---

habits that work to undermine the very success we wish to obtain. Our minds have catalogued the onset of every detrimental behavior that consigns us to our present condition. Therefore, the ability to change lies with that individual who is willing to perform introspection to identify and uproot those damaging patterns of thought that serve only to handicap our ability to succeed. Your future success depends on your courage to rid yourself of fear, doubt, and discouragement that continue to lead you down a path of apathy and procrastination. No danger can arise in rooting out bad principles.

One of the most difficult chains to break is that of dependency. The alteration process begins when we remove the training wheels of dependency on others. Whenever you begin to wean yourselves from that which is familiar, strong protest is usually the first result. We often protest loudest against that which we do not understand because the path to great wealth will take us through a process of being weaned off of bad habits. The moment you stop looking for others to become your knight in shining armor is the moment you can boldly realize your financial desires. Whenever you depend on the mercies of others, know that they will never provide you with an abundance of what you are hoping for. You will always be stuck at "just enough." It takes a certain mentality or way of thinking for a person to be an entrepreneur. In order to break away from co-dependency, you have to uproot what you have been taught about a thing so that you can install another operating system. By this, I am suggesting that everyone

> *Your philosophy of life will manifest in how you conduct your daily routine.*

has a philosophy that governs how he or she lives. Our philosophical view of the world dictates how we think about money, family, business, church, and physical health. Your philosophy of life will manifest in how you conduct your daily routine.

Some years ago, computers were purchased with basic operating software called DOS (Disk Operating System) that served as a template to enable other loaded programs to properly function and interface. DOS was very difficult to learn and was not at all user-friendly. Microsoft later developed a program called Windows. Windows is actually a graphical user interface that replaced the need to input commands with just a simple press on the mouse. In similar fashion, most people are operating according to an obsolete system that keeps them in a state of "Just Enough." Everything appears problematical with the old system. If people will divorce themselves from the mind set that suggests that all efforts toward achieving success must be hard, they will be able to overcome any level of difficulty in any situation. People need to be willing to change their operating system to one that is relevant and applicable for producing results not insults. The only difficulty in changing is changing.

> **The only difficulty in changing is changing.**

Seventy to seventy-five percent of America's millionaires are first generation millionaires. Despite increasing taxes, controls, and other stumbling blocks enforced by governmental agencies, the number of millionaires continues to grow and grow. How is it that America produces more millionaires than any other country? How is it that, in the world's richest nation, millions live their lives in poverty?

Many of these new millionaires did not have thousands in the bank before achieving success; they simply banked on their ideas. When you have the mentality of "just enough," you will never have enough for your dreams.

Riches may not bring happiness, but neither does poverty. Although wealth may not bring happiness, it brings a pretty close imitation of it. Most people have it all wrong when it comes to the subject of wealth. Wealth is not the same as income. If you make a good income each year and spend it all, you are not getting wealthier. Wealth is what you accumulate, not what you spend. Some people mistaken their reported financial net worth for their actual self-worth; thinking themselves to be worth a lot of money. In actuality, the money we own can never properly measure our true worth to society because a bogus balance sheet will always come up short. I don't need a lot of money to know my worth. My money value is not based on how much money I have, but how much talent and ability I am willing to exchange for it.

Wealth is, in many ways, simply a state of mind. An abundance of financial wealth should never be a factor for determining of how wealthy we truly are. Rather it is only a gauge to measure how well we have negotiated our talents and abilities in the marketplace for a compensatory wage. As a life coach to many men and women across this nation, my endeavor is to get individuals to begin to reassess their view of wealth and the talents that they possess. Whenever I consider helping a person in business or life, I always emphasize the establishment of a solid foundation. Strong foundations are always constructed from humble and fragile beginnings. The foundation is that set of principles that enable us to stand properly and allow us to reach our desired destinations. My goal, where people are concerned, is to cause them to focus on where they dreamed to be, from where they presently are.

The handout, get lucky, give-me-a-job mentality has kept too many people broke and unable to provide for themselves. When the strings are cut from just enough and you are tied to more than enough, it is an initial change of thinking not an increase of money. If you receive a financial increase without first having a new mental operating system, the increase will surely dwindle

> *When the strings are cut from just enough and you are tied to more than enough, it is an initial change of thinking not an increase of money.*

down to your level of "just enough" thinking. Therefore, a man must be willing to take risks if he is to achieve any sort of success. The person who waits until he is certain will wait forever. There is no risk involved when faith guides your efforts.

I typically warn against being too cautious when it comes to living life or investing for the future. To attempt to avoid risk at every turn leads to life never fully lived or explored. There will never arise a perfect moment to begin to pursue your dreams. Just as the direction of the wind is forever changing, so too are the conditions that drive all investment markets. You will be paralyzed by inactivity if you become overly concerned with potential stock market crashes or corporate fraud. If a farmer waits for the perfect, ideal season in which to plant his crops, the world would starve to death.

Break the cycle of just enough and replace it with a mentality of "More than enough." Don't let your future be controlled by chance; control your future by changing your financial philosophy. Throw your words and money into tomorrow so that when you arrive there, they will be waiting for you with a harvest of more than you initially threw in.

The Ten Commandments of Money

▼

Poverty is not a shortage of the supply of money,
but a shortage of information concerning it.
Mikel Brown

CHAPTER 7

The Ten Commandments of Money

A business executive was staying at a hotel and he decided to go to the vending machine at the end of the corridor. He stood staring at the items in the vending machine unable to decide on what he wanted. A young boy appeared and stepped in front of the man and began putting quarters into the machine. The boy dropped two, four, six, eight quarters. Finally the executive tapped the boy on the shoulder and said, "Son, you're putting way too much money into the machine." The boy turned to him and said, "Oh no, sir! See, the more money I put in, the more stuff I get out!"

Poverty is not a shortage of the supply of money, but a shortage of information concerning it. Your knowledge of money will either increase or limit your supply of it. You must begin to receive new and sound data about money so that the information in your head can increase the supply in your pocket. The subject of money is covered in every book of the bible, and it is mentioned directly or indirectly more times than any other subject. Love is mentioned about 281 times, but there are over 1300 scriptures that give reference to money. Obviously, God wants us to be fully aware of the potential of money so that we can appropriately apply its use.

Money has the potential of snaring and controlling people more than any other thing on earth, including sex. The power that money has over the lives of

> **You are the product of your information.**

people exists because they are more consciously aware of its commercial value than anything else they may own. There are two items that you cannot live without in this world, food and water and the other is money. Unless you farm your own food, you will starve if you don't have money to buy it. Ultimately, money is more essential than food in our society because with money you can buy all the food and water you need. On the other hand, food and water cannot buy money unless there is a shortage of it.

There are Ten Commandments for money that will help you to gain a proper perspective of it. If you do not have the knowledge to resist its powerful pull, it can cause even the best of people to abandon their integrity. Many accountants have justified stealing millions from their employers because they reasoned within themselves that a few dollars taken from a large sum of money would never be missed. So they surrendered to their suppressed greed and embezzled what was not theirs. Throughout every industry in society, people can relate their stories of hiring individuals whom they trusted only to be ripped off by the very ones to whom they gave jobs. On the other side of this experience are those who became rich and ruthless as a result of their theft. Money became the powerful tempter that enticed them to cast off all moral restraint or fear of legal repercussions in order to obtain that almighty dollar. We are not born knowing what is morally right. Certain moral imperatives must be taught to us at a very early age. You are the product of your information. Your system of morals derived from the principles your parents may or may not have taught you. Therefore, I believe that these Ten Commandments are needed in order to help a person deal with the success that may come from reading this book.

Commandment 1

Thou shall not worship money.

You are not designed to worship two gods; you are built to honor just one. You were created to be single-minded, not double minded. You are either going to be with the one you love, or you are going to love the one you're with. Both God and Money are portrayed, not as employers, but as masters. A man may work for two employers, but he cannot serve two masters. He will find it difficult to be equally loyal. We are taught to work for money instead of having money to work for us.

Greed reaches for any amount.

The bible gives us an interesting account of the life of Judas Iscariot, one of the original chosen followers of Jesus. At first, Judas fit in very well alongside the other eleven disciples. He starts as the one who handled the money, but we later discover that it was more like the money handled him. Money exposes hidden agendas and reveals the true condition of one's heart. Judas' made a choice to become enslaved to money, and because of his choice, he would suffer an ignominious death. Contrary to popular belief, Judas did not betray Jesus with a kiss. His betrayal was the revealing of Jesus' identity to the Jewish Temple authorities in exchange for 30 pieces of silver. The infamous kiss of death for which Judas is most noted was merely the method Judas used to expose the identity of Jesus. In Exodus 21:32 in the bible, Judas betrayed Jesus for the same amount of money that a slave could be procured. It was not about how much money was involved in the betrayal plot because he consistently stole more than that while he was the entrusted steward over the ministry finances. Regardless of whether he stole ten dollars or ten million dollars, Judas' downfall was his love of money. Greed reaches for any amount.

Commandment 2

> # *Thou shall not seek wealth.*

There is a particular scripture in the bible that suggests that if a person seeks to be rich then he cannot and will not be honest. Millions live unfulfilled and frustrated lives because they do not understand the truth about money. Success or failure depends on what you believe. In marriage, in health, in spiritual matters, and in finances, what you believe makes all the difference in the world. Money is an abstract commodity, an illusion. It is not what money is that interests me. I am only interested in the supremacy of its rule and the things it can do. With money we are able to negotiate, trade and exchange our way through life! Money is the basic method of communication between human beings. It is the only true universal language.

> *Money is the basic method of communication between human beings.*

Money represents power, influence, achievement and security. For this very reason money can be deceptive. When people are dragged into money's hypnotic spell, they feel as though it will solve all of their problems. With that type of thinking, it is no small wonder why people will do practically anything to get it. I believe firmly that honesty is still the best policy.

Commandment 3

Thou shall not hoard.

The wealthiest man that ever lived was King Solomon, the son of King David. Notice what he had to offer in Ecclesiastes 5:10 regarding man's vain preoccupation with money and wealth. In this verse he states, "Whoever loves money never has money enough; whoever loves wealth is never satisfied with his income. This too is meaningless."

Most people struggle unsuccessfully in their efforts to obtain vast sums of money, but they have not realized that success with money comes only at the end of this great struggle. If it were easy, anybody could do it. Success is success only because it relates to struggle. How can you have victory without conflict? The struggle you may presently have with money exists because you are trying to break loose from its powerful influence. As you gather more information about your true identity, people and things will lose their ability to control you. People hoard money

> *The struggle you may presently have with money exists because you are trying to break loose from its powerful influence.*

basically because they believe for some reason that it validates their worth or increases their importance in eyes of others. Money is a gauge to reveal the condition of your heart. What adversely affects a person is not the amount of money they make, but how much they love the money made.

Commandment 4

Thou shall not enter into debt.

Today, many people are having trouble coping with the amount of money they owe. They are overwhelmed by their financial obligations, and record numbers are filing bankruptcy. There is a scripture in the bible that essentially says, that the borrower is a slave to the lender. How true is this? I have seen both men and women with migraine headaches, ulcers and other ailments go to work because they could not afford to stay home. That, my friend, is modern day slavery.

Wisdom is the most important thing you can gain because with it you will have the proper insight of common sense to make balanced, informed decisions about how to manage money. Wisdom will teach you that debt is a monster that derives from our uncontrollable craving to buy things even if we cannot afford them. If the impulse within people to spend beyond their means were not so powerful, then debt would cease to exist as a major problem in society. Financial debt has kept more people from moving forward in business ventures than the lack of knowledge. Most people would love to be the employer, but they are unwilling to pay the price that accompanies the responsibility. Constant anxiety due to bills piling up on the kitchen counter serves as a reminder to too many would-be business owners that they must first deal with their debt before they should start a business. Debt may hinder you for a season, but it does not have the power to ultimately stop you. There are three things you can start now to help you get out of debt.

1. Negotiate with your debtors.
2. Make constant weekly, bi-weekly, or monthly payments.
3. When you receive a pay increase, don't make another bill; use it to pay off bills.

Commandment 5

> ## *Thou shall change thy belief about money.*

Five lies concerning money.

1. More money will cure my problems and make me more content.

Are you fully satisfied with the last salary increase you received? Probably not! Living the purpose driven life brings fulfillment, not the mere accumulation of possessions. If people would be honest, they would admit that it was the extra money that came into their lives that seemed to compound their problems. Money can lead you into your wilderness or you can lead your money into your promised land.

2. Money is irrelevant or immaterial.

Shelter, food, clothing, transportation, medical care, and education…what do they all have in common. It takes money to enjoy them all. If you think that money doesn't count, why then did Jesus have Judas as an accountant? If money doesn't count, what else are you going to count - your fingers? Money itself cannot clothe me. It cannot feed me, and neither can it house me. It is the tool that seems to fix and make the world go round and with it I can purchase all of life's necessities.

3. A person should not want to be financially successful.
This belief is stupid and downright absurd! The necessities of life demand finances. To merely have enough for us four and no more is robbing the human race. Money should never control your life, but be used merely as a tool to enhance it. You should desire more money so that you can buy quality items instead of purchasing things that will only fall apart after wearing it for only one evening. If you weren't supposed to make the money, then you wouldn't have it!

4. Some people have special gifts for wealth, while some are destined for poverty.
This kind of foolish thinking has destroyed the initiative, drive, and motivation in many would-be successful people throughout the world. The truth of the matter is that your hard work or lack of it has gotten you where you are today. God gives us all gifts. All have the gift to make money.

> *All have the gift to make money.*

5. It's better to give love rather than money because it is the love that counts.
This statement is also inconsistent with life in general. Love cannot pay your mortgage, but it can make you feel better. It is the cheap person who would choose to give love rather than money when money is what is needed. The acid test for true love is your willingness to give what you truly love.

Commandment 6

> ## *Thou shall invest with the expectation of receiving.*

Some people will dare to call this action and reaction a selfish desire. Selfishness exists whenever we seek to gain in life only at the expense of others. It is depriving from others what we do not withhold from ourselves. Capitalism is an economic system whereby the investment of capital and the economic means of production, land, labor, capital, and entrepreneurship are controlled by private individuals and corporations. The entire system of heaven and earth is established on this principle of exchange. I am revealing the secrets to kingdom prosperity. Your release determines your increase.

The next commandment is going to deal with acquiring the knowledge in order to create wealth. Since God gave us the ability to manufacture increase, what is the apparatus used and how can it be used to produce more increase? I have learned that God will not do for us what He has enabled us to do for ourselves. The one million-dollar question is a simple, how? God has given to you the power to produce wealth. This principle is used for everything in life. How much love I receive is dependent upon how much love I give. How much money I invest will result in how much money I receive.

Commandment 7

> ## *Thou shall give.*

What must be taught to people is the awesome blessing that is attached to our giving. Giving is the lever used to release and bring your increase. Giving is a principle that all businessmen should learn in order to help their business to prosper. Bill Gates gives hundreds of millions of dollars to charitable organizations annually. This principle is called the Law of Reciprocity. The two authors of *"Chicken Soup for the Soul"*

> *Giving is a principle that all businessmen should learn in order to help their business to prosper.*

series are people who believe in giving a tenth of their earnings to the church and other charitable organizations. As a result of their giving, *"Chicken Soup for the Soul"* has sold over 60 million copies. They report to make over 3 million a year in their deal with Hallmark Greeting Cards. I know many businessmen who give a tithe (tenth in Hebrew) to their church or synagogue. You may not fully understand this principle, but then again we don't fully understand much regarding many of the things we do. Start giving a tenth of your income to your church and begin to look for the return you will received. One business owner refused to enter into a partnership relation without his partner agreeing to give ten percent of their business earning. When asked why their business gave ten percent to the church they both attend, he said, "All of what our business has achieved is because of the Lord's blessings toward us. How could I not give back?"

Commandment 8

> ## Thou shall be trustworthy with thy money.

How much you have now has been predetermined by how

much you can handle. The supreme qualities required in a steward are fidelity and trustworthiness. There is no excuse for mishandling money or constantly bouncing checks. The mismanagement of your financial affairs demonstrates a lack of diligence and attention to detail. Furthermore, the mismanagement of ones personal financial affairs often means that the balance of ones life is also in a state of disrepair

> **Lasting wealth is always based on good stewardship.**

and mismanagement. An unwise person cannot be trusted with much because they refuse to heed sound instruction. Your ability to handle money is an accurate gauge for determining whether or not you can be corrupted by it. Large sums of money have eluded so many people because they have proved to be unfaithful stewards of the little money already in their care. The inability to faithfully manage small amounts of wealth will certainly disqualify you from handling larger estates. The mismanagement of what you presently have could possibly have disqualified you for what you could have had. Lasting wealth is always based on good stewardship.

Commandment 9

> **Thou shall believe that thou can be Wealthy.**

You must be fully persuaded that you can increase your income and improve your business for maximum profit. You must be completely convinced of this before you can go further. I know how it feels when you continue to make attempts to increase your income, only to discover that you are spending money on get-rich-quick schemes that sound good, but it leaves you with long hours and empty promises. All of your prior knowledge about money must be destroyed so that new knowledge can be received. "You don't have to believe every thought that comes into your mind, but you do have to have a thought to believe." *Mikel Brown*

Commandment 10

> # *Thou shall commit thyself to being Wealthy.*

This commandment is actually a state of being, not becoming. Your intrinsic value points to your internal treasure that is deep-seated. A gentleman spoke of how often he reads success stories of businesses and businessmen, but he failed to mention how many books he had read that discussed how they got "there". He wrote three books and three commercials that he's trying to sell to a well-known sport television conglomerate. In his spare time, he operates a small business. He feels as if he's made all the right contacts, and yet he wonders about getting "there."

> *Directions are not useful unless you know where you want to go.*

My question is simple. Where is "there"? What is your vision of "there"? You write books. You're a small business owner and an advertising copywriter. Which of these if any are you truly passionate about? If you try to do too many things, it will be difficult to do any of them well enough to be truly pleased with the results. Until you can clearly define where "there" is for you, it will be hard for you to make use of the information and experience you already possess. If you can organize your life around reaching that place called "there," then you can better focus on "there" as opposed to "where." Directions are not useful unless you know where you want to go. And you cannot choose worthy role models if you are not clear about who and what you want to be.

8

Creating Wealth
by Starting a Business

▼

It will cost you absolutely nothing to dream.
Mikel Brown

| CHAPTER 8 |

Creating Wealth
by Starting a Business

What's wrong with dreaming? Dreaming is the most inexpensive way to produce a business and review its potential. It will cost you absolutely nothing to dream. Your dreams can produce a profit if you will only believe in them. The motivation to start a business will always come to us from some inspiring source. Whether via daydreaming, an epiphany, or as a result of some word being spoken to us, the idea to pursue a particular business venture will motivate us from within and push us in the direction of tremendous success if we would simply heed the unction of that small voice within. I strongly believe in listening to powerful words from people who have endured the trials and tribulations of life only to emerge victorious.

Allow me to share an amazing story with you that I am certain you will find to be incredible. Trust me! I will not insult your intelligence by sensationalizing what I am about to share because advertisers and salespersons quickly lose my attention by presenting me with claims that are too good to be true. We all know that if something sounds too good to

---

be true, then odds are the claim is false.

I want to share with you the life stories of some wonderful people whom I have personally mentored and have walked them through the Path to Wealth process. Charles Newman and Tish Times are co-owners of NewTimes Staffing Company. Approximately six years ago, they were both employed at different staffing companies and they were both very intimately aware of the administrative and operational ins and outs of running a staffing company. They lacked nothing in terms of knowledge, but they did have a small problem when they decided to come together to form their own staffing company. They had no start up capital, office, or contracts. I suppose they could have gotten by without an office, some furniture, or active contracts, but to venture into such an endeavor without financial capital is typically a proposition that is most ill-advised. How can you go to a bank for a loan without the necessary collateral to begin the negotiating process? You don't! "Well then, how does one start a Staffing Company without money," you ask. Easy! Starting a business is the easy part; running it is something all together different.

> *Starting a business is the easy part; running it is something all together different.*

Most people only talk of starting a business because after they have weighed what they have against what is required, the resultant deficit is usually enough to nullify the intentions of most. If you really want to start a business and money seems to be your biggest obstacle, then simply start without it. You heard me right! This is exactly what the owners of NewTimes Staffing Company had to do. I like what Jonathan Winters once said, "I couldn't wait for success to come, so I went on without it." If you are always waiting for the right time and for all the necessary essentials to be in place, you will never accomplish your goals. I can recall saying to Charles and Tish, "With all of your experience and expertise in the area of staffing, why are you working for someone else?" To which they would usually reply: "We need an office." or "We need so much money." or "Taxes and insurance premiums are too high." My question to them was, "How many excuses (obstacles) are you going to put in your way." At that moment, they were pitted with having to make a decision. They both had to admit that their biggest hindrance was that instead of reviewing what they had, they were looking at what they lacked.

Tish would always mention to me how often she had read my book, *"Beyond Ordinary: Success is only a thought away,"* and how she had highlighted so many passages from it. I thought that it must not have done you any good because you refuse to start the business you believe that you're capable of running. I decided to sit down with Charles and Tish and take them through a step-by-step what-if scenario for starting their business without the money they needed. The first thing I said was "you do not need an office, but you do need a phone." Business people usually spend time on the phone not in an office. I assisted them in pooling together the necessary connections to help with developing their Human Resource Department, Accounting, and Proposals. Their only out-of-pocket expense at this point was for paper and meals. We all sat down and brainstormed the name

> *Business people usually spend time on the phone not in an office.*

of the business. I simply reasoned that since this business venture would be a partnership, simply take and combine the first syllable from Charles' last name, Newman, Tish's entire last name, Times, to create the catchy title, "NewTimes Staffing," After spending a few bucks to register the business, they were exited to be legally in business and for less than one hundred dollars. You cannot finish what you don't start!

An amazing thing happened once they had formed the company. They were then able to generate the contracts that produced the money they complained they did not have,

> **You cannot finish what you don't start!**

and they were able to locate the personnel to staff their company. This, mind you, was only made possible once Charles and Tish flushed their excuses and began pursuing their dream of being business owners. I must admit, however, that their first in business experience was full of surprises and unexpected challenges. With the fortitude to begin and their faith in God, their company has received staffing contracts thus far as small as three hundred dollars to as much as 1.5 million dollars. By the way, I failed to mention that Charles and Tish both had to leave the security of their jobs so that they could pursue their dreams. How would you like your income to go from 0 to 1.5 million in less than one year?

What is your dream business? What are you passionate about doing but do not have a clue as to begin? Have you ever sat down on your living room couch and daydreamed of owning your own business? Statistically, 8 out of 10 people have voiced their thoughts of one day owning a business. Some have thought of parlaying their idea into a franchise operation, while others have thought of starting or buying an existing business. Whatever the case may be, having a business can move you a lot quicker up the financial ladder than working for a company that will only give you a nominal wage.

If you allow someone to decide on the size of your world, they will always make it too small. You are not being selfish

> **If you allow someone to decide on the size of your world, they will always make it too small.**

if you would like to work for yourself. Owning your own business will afford you certain tax advantages that otherwise would never be offered to you. But this is not the only reason for starting a business. Just the fact that you can be the one to determine your income potential and how many hours you're going to work is reason enough for me.

My publishing company published a book for a person who is a West Point grad and has developed programs for U.S Army Missile System. He worked for a company that pays him peanuts compared to what they are getting. If the company you work for contracted with another firm for the use of your skills for two hundred dollars an hour but only paid you thirty dollars an hour, how would such an arrangement make you feel? I know how I would feel cheated! "Why entertain thousands when you can consider millions", I said to him. You can start your own consulting business and make millions instead of thousands. Here is a person with all the right credentials, but with very little initiative and motivation needed to make things happen. He displayed these qualities for his job, but wrestled when it came to doing it for himself. When a person says that they are content with their salary, just ask them, why then, do they want to get more money.

You are built with the capacity for more, but many settle for less. Some people think that they have to deserve what they get by doing something good. You don't get what you deserve, you get what you take. There are many good people in the world who are

> ## You are built with the capacity for more, but many settle for less.

being treated badly by others. Companies will take advantage of anyone who would allow them to. The sooner you learn this, the better off you will see that you are without them. Since my company published his first book on Architectural Development, I assumed the responsibility to become a launching pad for his endeavors. I have a mandate to be a guide to helping people to walk the Path to Wealth. Sometimes, the price is rewarding while at other times it is labor intensive. With this person having all the raw material, I became his coach in business.

We sat down and brainstormed over a few ideas concerning all that he could do. I recall asking him whether anyone else could do his job. He let out a sigh and said, "I developed 75% of the architectural development programs and I am the only one who does it for the company I work for and the only one with the experience that companies within the Defense contracting industry will hire. Armed with that information, we launched his company and discovered that he did not have to go far for his first consulting job. He is sought after by large companies. He worked his first deal out by refusing to accept an offer to work for a company with a defense contract and was brought on as a consultant. He already has one contract of over $110,000 and several other contracts pending, which are in the range of $120,000 to $500,000. He has already surpassed his previous income level with his first contract. And just think, it started with just a dream and a mentor. It's a great thing to believe in yourself, but an even greater thing when someone else believes in you.

> ### It's a great thing to believe in yourself, but an even greater thing when someone else believes in you.

What does it take to make a dream come true? Few people who aspire to be self-sufficient ever realize their dreams. Some fear the unknown while most are simply confused by the many options available to them. As a result, many dismiss great opportunities because of the necessary information to wade through the excessive resources that exist regarding business start-up. The key to overcoming this dilemma is by heeding the counsel of an informed coach or mentor. "What happens if my dream gets deferred? What happens if my voice goes unheard? Does it simply fade to gray? I will not allow my dreams to dry up and become nothing more than a "raisin in the sun." as *Langston Hughes would say.* Never miscalculate the power of your dream. Continue to pursuit it until you find the winning strategy that will end your contest. I've learned that as long as you are exchanging blows, you can never be declared the loser. If your opponent decides not to come out for another round, you simply move on to the next one.

There are hundreds of thousands of successful entrepreneurs fueling the economy, creating jobs and launching innovative products and services that will propel the United States economy further into the 21st century. There are many successful entrepreneurs who have a tremendous amount of energy and who really love what they do. These people are recognized as having the same qualities and desire. Serious entrepreneurs cannot afford to

> # Know your strengths and weaknesses.

think small. They must maintain a big-thinkers mentality or their world will shrink. As a business owner, you are constantly being stretched, bent, and sometimes broken. But entrepreneurs are like Timex Watches that take a licking but they keep on ticking.

My most serious advice to anyone who is considering going into business for themselves is, START! **Strategize Thought Approaches for Reward Tactics**. What I mean by this is that you must strategize your thoughts and approaches for reward tactics. Think of ways your business can be deliberately and immediately rewarded by using tactics that will ensure great repeat business. Below are a few things you can do for your business or product.

1. Set up a permanent board of advisers.
2. Use focus groups to compare products.
3. Question customers on an ongoing basis.
4. Make benefits stand out.
5. Budget for cost overruns and unexpected expenses.
6. Team up with well-backed financial partners.
7. Offer a service, not a product.

Put things in place before you actually start your business and you will see things fall into place. Know your strengths and weaknesses. Do not be afraid to solicit advice from well-respected associates.

Eight Things Wealthy People Do that Average People Won't Do

▼

*The rich see opportunities
to work and invest their money,
and in their ideas*

Mikel Brown

CHAPTER 9

Eight Things Wealthy People Do that Average People Won't Do

Those with enormous wealth can influence the environment around them, and they have not failed in their attempts to do so. Those without wealth have to simply adapt to their environment. In the last twenty-five years, the share of total wealth held by the top 5% of the population has risen from 16 to over 21 percent of total wealth. That top 5 percent now owns as much market wealth as the bottom 60 percent. Why does there exist such a disparity between the haves and have-nots? High School diploma recipients have more than doubled and the number of college graduates has risen by a factor of almost four times over the past twenty years. As the education level rises in this country, one would assume that income levels would rise as well. But this has not been the case. What can account for this discrepancy? Our universities are not teaching students to become entrepreneurs. Rather, they are instilling in students the desire to become high-paid indentured servants. People do not normally become very rich by placing their money in a savings account that only yields one percent or less. The rich see opportunities to work and invest their money, and in their ideas.

The only reason why some people are not wealthy is that they are unwilling to endure the struggles to qualify for the prize of success. People are people good, bad, and indifferent. No individual owns the market on talent and ability. We all possess certain innate gifts that enable us to do some things better than others. None of us was born predisposed to be wealthy or poor. But there are many people who love to justify their station in life by choosing to believe that they were born without the advantages that others seem to have. Yet, they settle for being neither rich nor poor, but average. Average individuals love to play it safe. They will shoot an arrow at a tree and then draw the target around it. They live without goals for fear that they may not accomplish them. As I point out the seven things that wealthy people do, ask yourself this question; "Am I willing to do those things and take a risk?"

1. Wealthy people refuse to work for others.

Working for someone else is out of the question for these self-motivated people. They enjoy the liberty of being able work without the hassle of someone watching over their

> **What you don't lose you can use.**

shoulder. They have never truly been comfortable working for someone because their initiative and self-determination causes them to be at constant loggerheads with their bosses. Insecure managers usually prevent such self-driven individuals from coming into contact with company owners for fear that the owners might recognize certain qualities in that individual and consequently promote him or her. The unwillingness in some, to work for anyone should not be construed as egotism. On the contrary, they are simply individuals with vision and goals of their own, and whose own future cannot be neglected because of the time-wasting attachments to the dreams of others.

2. Wealthy people work best under stress.

Stress for average people causes them to fall apart. Whereas, the wealthy use life's pressures to bring out their best. These purpose-driven individuals view eight hours of sleep as an unnecessary interruption from the pursuit of their dreams. A poll taken of the dominant characteristics of the wealthy revealed that these highly motivated people slept an average of only four hours a night. Not much sleep when you think about! There are times when, because of the number of ideas racing in my mind, I simply could not sleep. At times like this, it helps if you are disciplined enough to jot down those ideas because the odds of losing them to memory is great. You will be surprised by the wealth of ideas that come to you late at night. Remember! What you don't lose you can use.

> *Wealthy people are seemingly inured to the pressures of life that seemingly slow the progress of ordinary individuals.*

Wealthy people are seemingly inured to the pressures of life that seemingly slow the progress of ordinary individuals. To them, pressure is a normal part of life. They view pressure as a time for change from lesser to greater, smaller to bigger. Pressure does not make the man; it only exposes him for what he already is. You will never go far if you based life on your good intentions. Learn how to deal with the pressures of life, and you will be able to deal in business.

> *Learn how to deal with the pressures of life, and you will be able to deal in business.*

3. Wealthy people are usually motivated by their imagination and dreams.

Those who have labored to amass great wealth are usually quite astute in business as well as in life. Their ability to move forward despite opposition lies in the fact that they are guided by a clear and powerful vision. The ability to see into the future toward one's dream is a quality that forces self-made millionaires to forge ahead when everything around them is screaming quit. The ability to dream and the great pictures formed by wild imaginations are all the evidence they need to stay the course to achieve their objectives. Most people give up on the promise of their tomorrows because they have no photograph of the future that frames their hope. Successful business people do not easily give up on their dreams, especially since the pictures they carry within of their success is too precious to simply discard.

4. Wealthy people are willing to make opportunities where there aren't any.

If you truly want to know why these people are where they are financially... they are willing to do everything you are unwilling to do. There's a difference

> *There's a difference between looking for an opportunity and making one.*

between looking for an opportunity and making one. Where there is no door to go through, successful people will stop looking for one so that they can create a door. You cannot survive long in business in a capitalistic society by being passive and afraid to confront challenges. Success does not happen by accident and neither is wealth created out of thin air. The problem with most people is that they would rather wait for someone else to give them a break. Wake up! You are that rich person with all the potential to build wealth. You must become a pioneer and lead the way for others to follow.

5. Wealthy people do not see quitting as an option.

Many people take great comfort in being able to simply throw in the towel and give up on their dreams when times are tough. Our ancestors understood full well that as the individual thrives, so thrives the nation. This country did not prosper without the sacrifices of many. Wars tried this nation's right to exist, and the countless investment of inventions and ideas that have all served to make America the most powerful and prosperous nation the world has ever known. Wars were fought to preserve our right to enjoy the spoils of capitalism and to secure this nation's freedom. With similar fortitude have countless men and women been able to defy uncharted territory to seize their wealth and prosperity. They realized the price that had to be paid, but found the courage to persevere knowing that others would benefit from their tenacity. Only those who possess the

> *Only those who possess the courage to fight through the lean and tough times are able to enjoy the fruit of wealth and prosperity.*

courage to fight through the lean and tough times are able to enjoy the fruit of wealth and prosperity.

6. Wealthy people are willing to be disliked or criticized.

There are many people who would like to enter your world for no other purpose than to stop you from succeeding. There is no reason why you should allow anyone to cast a shadow over your ability to make money. Unfortunately, we sometimes do. Friends, family members, and associates can all qualify as invalidators. Invalidators are people who operate in our lives for no other purpose than to

> ***There is no reason why you should allow anyone to cast a shadow over your ability to make money.***

hinder us from achieving our success. Invalidators are the first to point out why your ideas will never work. Most of us can detect when people are trying to derail us from the path to our goals. But we may not be so quick to oppose the counterproductive efforts of invalidators when our friends and family members are the perpetrators of such evil plots. They will give you fifty reasons why you are not qualified for a particular job, while all the while maintaining their friendship. You may be their friend, but rest assured they are certainly not yours! People with focus and direction have no problem severing toxic relationships. They don't mind the criticism that is likely to

> ***People with focus and direction have no problem severing toxic relationships.***

ensue because they are persuaded of who they are and what they must to do succeed in life. To much of my surprise, I discovered that along with wealth comes criticism. You cannot have one without the other.

> **Wealth is not greed; greed is not wealth.**

Athletes are always criticized by their fans. Their every action is closely scrutinized and examined under the microscope of public opinion. Critics who don't have the guts to attempt what you actually achieve will always sit on the sidelines yelling, "I wish I could get out there and show him what to do!" Your biggest critics will always know the least about what you do, but take it upon themselves to offer you the most input. Wealthy people are often criticized by those who are not, for no other purpose than because they are not. People who are not wealthy usually hold the view that rich people are selfish, greedy pigs. Okay, maybe I took this one too far. Wealth is not greed; greed is not wealth. Wealthy people do not object to losing friends; average people wail over them.

7. Wealthy people are usually people who are willing to give.

A strong financial sense and a strong moral sense go hand-in-hand. I believe that many investors and business people are

> **A strong financial sense and a strong moral sense go hand-in-hand.**

tired of the "greed is good" and or "profit at any cost" stereotypes that most people hold regarding the investment or business industries. People want to feel good about making money. They like the fact that their money can do some good for charitable organizations such as churches, the Feed the Children Program, or the Red Cross. Sometimes the best way to approach heaven is by standing on your wallet. Wealthy people are the main contributors to charitable organizations. The average person gives less then 3% of his income to organizations that depend on freewill gifts for support. This may be part of the reason why average people remain average while wealthy people continue to grow wealthier. The truly wealthy always share the wealth which they have made.

> *Sometimes the best way to approach heaven is by standing on your wallet.*

8. Wealthy people are not indifferent toward having to work long hours.

Oftentimes, long hours are necessary especially when one is initially starting a business and this is one great deterrent for average people. Average people love their 9 to 5 hours too much to sacrifice their usual couch experience. Yet they would love to experience the pleasures that wealthy people are privileged to enjoy without having to extract from their retirement investment in order to do so. Some things just take time and it can prove to be time well spent. People of success are not clock watchers. They would prefer to iron out the details of a new proposal·rather than to go home to watch television. It's not that they are unwilling to spend time with their family, because in many cases these people spend quality time. Quantity is not as important as quality, if all you're going to do is stay home and not communicate with your family. People of wealth are able to take long vacations with their family, while visiting exotic islands and taking Disney Cruises to the Bahamas. Average people are stuck with borrowing money to go visit Aunt Susie and Uncle Joe in Florida. Instead of flying, they get a rental vehicle and spend much of their vacation time driving instead of vacationing. One way or another, if you don't spend time wisely in preparing for your future, you will eventually end up wasting time while engaging in unproductive activities.

The mark of a truly successful person is how much he or she is ultimately able to give back to the people that helped them to succeed. No one person can ever say that he or she made it on his or her own merit. Money changes hands because people buy products. If no one bought into your dream, all you would have is a non-productive dream. You are the gardener who must plant his seeds so that what is produced will ultimately feed nations. I've learned that the most individually successful people are actually the greatest servants of the common good. If successful and wealthy people fall short in the area of giving, I can say with certainty that those people will lead miserable lives. If you only live for yourself, what good are you to others? Wealth is a blessing from above. The challenge lies in making money, but the greatest pleasure lies in sharing it!

> *The challenge lies in making money, but the greatest pleasure lies in sharing it!*

10

Follow that Dream

▼

*It is not the material of the dream that matters;
it is what the dream does that you commit to.*
Mikel Brown

CHAPTER 10

Follow that Dream

A dream is a series of images, ideas, and emotions that occur in certain stages of sleep. It is a state of suspended abstraction. In fact, a dream is a vision that appears to us without our invite. Simply put, a dream is a movie of thoughts and images shown while asleep and, at times while awake. Some people see them as hope while I view them as targets. A person must not be intimidated about dreaming something that appears out of reach. You will never grow unless you attempt to accomplish that which lies just beyond your reach.

Dr. Martin Luther King, Jr. dared to share his dream with the world, and he paid the ultimate price for his dream. The vision that he carried inside cost him his life, but his dream regarding humanity was greater than the life he was willing to capitulate. Your dream is linked to your destiny. Your destiny is greater than any pain and suffering you may have to endure to realize your dream. There will be frustrations and doubts along the way, but if determined, you will make it to the end. Do not allow others to cause you to abort your

---

dreams with their negativity. You must endeavor to keep the dream alive despite the opposition that will inevitably come to derail you from your journey.

In real life, no one is allowed to fight to a draw. We must emerge from our struggles as either winners or losers. You must decide for yourself how important your dream is. The weight of your decision rests upon your shoulders, and you alone must carry the load. However, if you determine that your dream is worth the fight, the fruit of success will validate your struggles in the end.

> **Dream as if tomorrow will never come...live as if you have one today to fulfill it.**

I have never heard of anyone achieving great success without having to endure great opposition. I wish I could say that life will be "smooth sailing" from the moment you receive a dream until the time you realize it. But such is never the case. The truth of the matter is that you will not know hell on earth until you begin to pursue your dreams. Those bent on destroying your dreams will not manifest until you become serious about pursuing your destiny. This happens with every person who struggles with reaching out to enjoy brighter tomorrows while having to deal with issues of past failures and insecurities. You can know a person for years, but you will never discover their hidden dislikes and jealousies of you until you begin to articulate to them your intentions to pursue your dreams of greatness.

"Why does a dream cause some relationships to sever," one may ask. Jealousy of you will always appear in the hearts of some people close to you as you begin to reach for the greater things in life that they fail to. As you reach far beyond yourself, you will leave your present station of mediocrity and anyone who is anchored to it. As a result, most people will not know how to identify with the new you. In essence, the gulf that now exists between you and them is usually too wide to allow old relationships to persist. Eleanor Roosevelt once said, "The future belongs to those who believe in the beauty of their dreams." You must dream as if tomorrow will never come…live as if you have one day to fulfill it.

> *The person who may not understand why you are willing to climb so high or reach so low, or walk so far, is someone who has never followed their dream.*

Who determines where you live, and who selects the car you drive? Who has been given authority to make choices for your life? Who and what established the prerequisites for your success? Is education a basic requirement or does money turn out to be the deciding factor in determining how far you will go? I can assure you of this one important thing: that talent will win over disadvantages, and the will to win will certainly overcome obstacles. Life is very short, and within its content are delays and stoppages, twists and turns, and difficulties. Therefore, you must be deliberate with your aim and narrow in on the target of your pursuit.

I have learned that opposition sometimes comes from within. This internal warring may be the result of your personal experiences, the way your parents raised you, or your belief system formed by influences of significant people in our lives. Just as you can be your greatest asset, you can also *be* your greatest enemy. You must be willing to look within so that you can deal with those issues that can sabotage your success. Focus on reprogramming yourself from within so that your circumstances will begin to change without. Do not allow people to visit you with their unsolicited, negative opinions of your dreams. I assure you that you will have enough to deal with regarding your own self-assessments when the pressures begin to mount.

I am reminded of a story of a young kid who purchased a pair of ice skates so that he could learn how to skate. In the process of his learning, he fell repeatedly. A gentleman sitting on the side felt sympathy as he watched this young kid. He was moved as he saw the boy's tears and the blood that flowed from the cuts sustained as a result of his constant falling. He skated over to the young kid, helped him up while brushing him off, and said, "Son, why don't you quit and come off the ice before you seriously hurt yourself." The young kid looked up at the gentleman and said, "I didn't buy these ice skates to learn how to quit; I bought them to learn how to skate." The person who may not understand why you are willing to climb so high or reach so low, or walk so far, is someone who has never followed their dream.

> *Specially selected words can cause a person to redirect their whole focus.*

Surely, you have a dream! There is a dream residing in your heart that you would love to experience more than anything in the world. My mother informed me of the time when I was a kid that she would often ask me, "Mikel, what do you want to do when you grow up?" "I want to travel the world." I would say. Well, I have fulfilled a portion of that desire by traveling three-quarters around the globe on speaking engagements. My personal dream has always been to be a businessman and an author. I had no particulars about the kind of business I wanted to own. I just knew that I wanted to own my own business and author books. For much of my early years I thought that I would never have the chance to those longings. No one informed me that I would face challenges that would almost wipe me out. After experiencing a devastating divorce and a diminishing income, my dream became more nebulous than ever before. I am certain that my critics watched with anticipation to see what my next move would be. I had a visit from a gentleman whom I still regard as a personal mentor. He did not come to me with handouts or to help me have a pity party. He had a simple yet timely God-sent word of encouragement that came at a critical juncture in my life. He said, "Get up and stop giving these people something to talk about!" I wept! I thanked him for coming to encourage me, but I realized that I must now encourage myself. I had allowed myself to become the victim, and I had begun to have my own private pity parties. It was at this point that I began to take inventory of my life and to again push in the direction of my dreams. It is amazing how specially selected words can cause a person to redirect their whole focus. For this very reason, I believe strongly that we should all surround ourselves with people who can be to us coaches and mentors. I developed an entire series of booklets called "The Pocket Motivator" in order to help others to get over the hump of discouragement and back onto the path to reaching their dreams.

Does it seem like your dreams are so far ahead of you that you need the space shuttle just to get within viewing distance? Well, if you possess the ability to lease the space shuttle to chase your dreams, I can tell you now, you're already moving in the right

> *It is difficult to pursue your dream when your car is in park.*

direction. It is difficult to pursue your dream when your car is in park. You may be a gourmet cook with great culinary skills. But without an established place of your own, the general public may never know the priceless value of your talent. Open your own restaurant; it need not remain a distant thought. When you begin to taste even the smallest amount of success where your dreams are concerned, you will be hungry for more.

I know an African American gentleman who owns a car dealership in New Mexico. He once worked for the father of a friend of mine who is now the CEO of the largest Mercedes, Volvo, Lexus, and Acura dealership in the Southwest. The

> *Some of your friends and associates will laugh at your dreams until they see you living them.*

African American car dealer did not have a lot of money. He did not have a degree from Harvard University. All he had was a dream to own and operate his own car dealership. The odds were against him, and they were stacked high. Does it matter what the odds are when your dream gives you the winning edge? Odds are only estimations, but a dream is authentic material when you believe it. Some may argue this point, but I assure you, it is true. His dream was the material of reality, and that was the reason he pursued it. He now has a thriving dealership in an area where no other businesses wanted to be. Of course he had some loving relatives that wanted nothing but the best for him. But he also had to plow through all the critics, including some family members who did not embrace his dream. How is it that your failure can bring happiness to your critics? If your success can sadden others, I say to those people, "Get a life!" Do not spend your time answering your critics. Just succeed, and that will do all the talking for you. Some of your friends and associates will laugh at your dreams until they see you living them.

How to Buy a $100,000 Acre of Land for $6,800

Think back to one of those times in your life when everything went right. With total confidence, you visualized the outcome you wanted, and it happened! Then there are those times when an obstacle gets in the way; you pushed, worked hard, and made sacrifices, but still came up short. What do you do when what you have reached for has moved out of your reach? In some cases the goal does not seem to move just a few inches away, but light years out of reach. Do you work harder, doing anything and everything in your power to overcome the obstacle? How much longer do you work to overcome it? Will it take another month, a year or more? I know the feeling. I also know the many mental battles that must be waged when you see others accomplishing their goals while yours seem to move further away.

> **If you refuse to yield to disappointment, you will find fulfillment dancing with opportunity, perseverance and preparation.**

One day as I was preparing to leave my hotel room for a speaking engagement in Camden, Delaware, I discovered that I had inadvertently left my cufflinks at home. The only shirts I brought were shirts with French cuffs. I frantically looked several times in my luggage to make sure that they were not hiding somewhere in one of the small compartments. The first thing I thought of was not finding another pair of cufflinks, but going to the Wal-Mart directly across the street for a dress shirt with button cuffs. Wal-Mart did not save the evening for me; but the ability to adapt to the unexpected. After collecting my thoughts, I simply strolled across the street, purchased a shirt, ironed it, left for my speaking engagement and delivered a dynamic message.

People do not want to hear how bad your day is going. They want to hear of how you turned your misfortune into a fortune. Success principles do not make distinctions between race, gender, educational level, or the rich and poor. They will work for anyone who will dare to use them and make them applicable to life's situations. I know you are anxious to hear how I purchased A One Hundred Thousand-Dollar Acre of land for only Sixty Eight Hundred Dollars. Patience please! If you are ever going to succeed financially, domestically, and spiritually, you must learn to allow patience to perform her perfect work in you.

> *Success principles do not make distinctions between race, gender, educational level, or the rich and poor.*

Oftentimes, my wife and I will share our dreams with one another and, to my surprise we once had the same dream about owning at least an acre of land to build our dream house on. We have had our dream house painted on the canvas of our mind for several years, but we needed land in a certain area in order to build it. So what did we do? We went searching for land that we knew would be of ample size to accommodate our dream home. Land is usually quite expensive when searching for the size plot we had in mind. One of our challenges was finding land in an area where the homes were at least 5000 square feet. We did not want to construct a large house in an area that would immediately depreciate our new home's value. Therefore, we had to be both patient and wise, avoiding the effects of continual frustration that resulted from our prolonged search. If you refuse to yield to disappointment, you will find fulfillment dancing with opportunity, perseverance and preparation.

One day I was driving alone, looking for land so that I could surprise my wife with some good news. I discovered a half-acre lot that I did not necessarily like, but was thinking of settling for it to end our prolonged agony. I spoke with the owner, and she was willing to sell the land for $80,000. The price was high, but I was mentally exhausted, physically drained and too weary to negotiate. I was in no mood to antagonize anyone. I went home to rejuvenate my strength, sharpen my negotiating skills and I fell asleep. This may not sound deep to you, but it was deep for me; deep sleep. I needed to rest my brain and take a load off. A good night's rest can restore mental alertness and rekindle the fire of desire. The key to getting ahead is setting aside eight hours a day for work and eight hours a day for sleep, and making sure they are not the same eight hours.

After regaining control of my faculties, I decided not to settle. We had decided that was not the land we really wanted, and especially not at that ridiculous price. I regard negotiating to be one of my strengths. As far as I'm concerned, everything is negotiable! I will negotiate the price of a McDonald's Happy Meal if I feel that I am receiving bad service. Well, soon after that bizarre experience, I ran across a one-acre site that had recently been filled in with dirt in order to level the land. The owner lived in a 5000 plus square foot home directly across the street from the property. She had recently experienced a divorce and was awarded the land and was now willing to sell it. Unfortunately for me, she was a realtor and builder. To add insult to injury, she was more interested in selling her home than the land. The

> *Overcome the temptation to settle when you know you can do better.*

divorce had caused this woman to become very shrewd about business. Her price for the land was a firm $95,000. I attempted everything in the book to get her to sell the property to me at a much cheaper price. I wanted this land so bad that I was almost willing to give her the asking price. If you cannot walk away from a deal that is not a win-win for both parties, you will lose your edge to negotiate. Later, she informed me that a church was interested in purchasing the land to build a parsonage for their pastor. I thought to myself, "I heard that line before." Well, it was true, and she consummated a deal with the Pastor for fifty thousand dollars down, and she financed the remaining amount for five years. My hopes of owning this ideal piece of land now seemed more unattainable than ever before.

I regrouped and continued my search with a greater fervor. Jonathan Winters, comedian/actor, once said, "I could not wait on success, so I went on ahead without it." Learn how to expose concealed opportunities by creating them. Some things are not meant to be hidden from you, they are hidden for you. God will hide them and you must seek them out. It is like playing the game you enjoyed as a child called hide and go seek. Whatever your dream is, you must believe that it is already in existence. You simply have to go out and find it.

My unquenchable fire of desire and relentless drive led me to an acre of land that proved to be a dream come true. My wife and I drove down to city hall to retrieve the records on this particular property to identify its owners. After receiving the information, I discovered that the owner was no longer living in the city where I reside. Therefore, I called 411 to get the scoop on this family and my investigation landed me in state of Arizona. I was able to reach the owner via telephone and proceeded to inquire about the land. They told me that they no longer owned the property because the bankruptcy court held it. I informed them of the taxes that were owed on the property and that the city records indicated that they were still the owners. The wife vehemently argued her case that she informed the attorney who represented her in the bankruptcy proceeding about the taxes owed, and her attorney informed her that he had taken care of it. "Can you give me the attorney's name so that I can investigate this problem further?" I asked. She gladly volunteered the information, and I was able to continue my pursuit. I attempted to reach the attorney but was only able to speak to his assistant. After I told her why I was calling, I asked her whether she would look into her files and provide me with whatever information she could. A week had passed and I still had not heard a word from her. I called again and inquired about the bankruptcy file on this couple. This time she stated that the files were no longer kept at their office but in a warehouse where they keep case files five years and older. Her lack of initiative and failure to respond to my inquiries was causing me to become very impatient. But I did not voice my displeasure with her effort or lack thereof because I needed an ally, not an enemy. And she was all I had.

> *Learn how to expose concealed opportunities by creating them.*

"Are you familiar with this case?" I asked the assistant. "Yes I am," she replied. I said to her that only a good assistant could remember cases that most attorneys choose to forget. I stressed the point that this couple was now in their seventies, the husband was disabled by the

> *Tell a person their faults and they will despise you. Stroke their ego and they will bend over backwards for you.*

effects of suffering a stroke, and they were on a fixed income. The taxes had not been paid in over twelve years, and they have continued to receive threatening letters from the city for a plot of land that they thought they no longer owned. This lady went right to work, and it only took a few days for her to return my call. I thought that this treasure hunt would end, but I soon discovered that it led to yet another clue. "The Bankruptcy Judge who sat on the bench has the warranty deed to the property," she explained.

I felt like saying, 'Here we go again.' However, this time it was not as difficult getting the information that I needed. I attempted to contact the Judge but could only reach his assistant. After explaining everything to her, I made this amazing discovery. If the property that was surrendered in bankruptcy court is not sold in order to settle the individual's debts, it is automatically returned to the owner. When I informed the owners of this, they were very troubled. Because what they had assumed concerning the land ended up being false. The wife of the owner asked me if there was a way that I could get a copy of the warranty deed for them. I gladly obliged them, went to the city's tax appraisal office, and paid for a copy of the warranty deed. After policing the document, she asked me if I would be interested in paying the taxes and owning the land. Trying to keep from sounding over elated about the offer, I informed her that my wife and I were interested in the land to build our new home.

My friend, the taxes were approximately $2900.00 and climbing. I could have escaped with only paying the taxes, but I wanted to help them by offering to give them an additional amount. I personally prepared the sales forms, faxed them to her husband, and he signed them and faxed them back to me. I quickly employed the services of a title company to ensure that the property was clear and unencumbered from all liens and that, in fact, they were the owners of the land. I never had to leave my desk to make and close this deal. This dear lady was so encouraging that she commended me for my research and diligence. She made known to me that other realtors had called her to purchase the land, but as soon as she would inform them that the land was in bankruptcy they would not inquire any further into the matter.

> *You can cause your dreams to happen if you are willing to do what others are too lazy to do.*

I really believe that this dear lady was simply rewarding me for my relentless efforts and as a result, decided to sell us the land at a ridiculously low price. At closing, I presented a cashier's check for $6880 for approximately an acre of land that could have easily sold for over $100,000. Some people may call it luck, others may even claim fate, but I say that I simply "Followed that Dream." Life is not an accident, nor is it a rehearsal. You can cause your dreams to happen if you are willing to do what others are too lazy to do. If I was down, why should I wait for a passerby to help me get up when I can get up all by myself? Getting up is the natural thing to do for anyone who ever actually falls down. Stop waiting for your ship to come in; build one. Put your gears in drive and Follow that Dream.

> *Stop waiting for your ship to come in; build one.*

Tips on Winning Ideas for Financial Increase

▼

You don't have to know how to do a thing well;
you just have to know what to do.
Mikel Brown

CHAPTER 11

Tips on Winning Ideas for Financial Increase

Y ou don't have to know how to do a thing well; you just have to know what to do. God has designed us in such a manner that causes us to continually seek ways to release our creativity. With eyes that stretch to see, ears that hearken to hear, and hands that clamor to touch, we seek both to absorb the wondrous beauty of our environment and to contribute to it. Similarly, we possess an inherent need to reach out into our environments in order to find ways to increase the wealth that we already have. Wealth must exercise its ability to grow or else it will be reduced to its lowest common denominator – poverty.

There is one characteristic that you cannot locate within the make-up of a winner. Try hard as you may, you will not find a "quitter's" mentality in the heart of a winner. The journey to your success is not over when you experience defeat; it is only over when you decide to quit. Life will present you with many opportunities to give up on your dreams. In trying times, too many people resort to quitting as the ideal alternative method to cope with challenge. People who have tasted the thrill of victory understand that such feeling is only made possible by overcoming setbacks.

> **The journey to your success is not over when you experience defeat; it is only over when you decide to quit.**

You can usually determine the disposition of a person's heart by the position of their head. People who have consigned themselves to defeat, move through life with hung down heads. Have you ever walked into a room to find an exciting game on television and wondered who was winning? As you watch the teams playing, it will become very apparent to you in a short period of time just which team is losing. The body language of players will reveal who is winning and who is losing. The moment you begin to wear a loser's disposition is the very moment your dream stops living. You must neutralize the power of whatever or whoever it is that tries to snuff the life out of your dreams. Fighting to overcome challenges is simply a part of life, and your dreams are worth the fight to win.

Don't allow your positive attitude to lose altitude. A person with soaring enthusiasm usually operates from the position of the predator. If you lack enthusiasm, you will exercise the mental posture of the prey. Keep your excitement level riding high! Don't be concerned with failing. To fail is not necessarily a choice, but quitting is. If you choose to never quit, eventually your failure will turn into success. Quitting today is an injustice to your tomorrow! Absolutely no one can stop you,

> **To fail is not necessarily a choice, but quitting is.**

but you. Stop complaining about your financial situation! Stop feeding your doubt images of discouragement. YOU CAN CHANGE ANYTHING IN YOUR LIFE, IF YOU WANT TO! It's as simple as repositioning the furniture in your home.

Don't bankrupt your mind by denying it new thoughts that can create new ways of doing things. Feed it what it desperately needs. If things are not the way I want them, I am not going to sit around and wait for things to get better. I am going to make things better. Procrastination is the fertilizer that allows difficulty to grow out of control. The longer you procrastinate in making a move toward a better life, the harder it will appear to be.

> *Procrastination is the fertilizer that allows difficulty to grow out of control.*

MOUNTAINS ARE NOT TOO BIG TO MOVE AND MOVING THEM IS NOT TOO HARD TO DO!

The only thing stopping you from changing your situation or starting your business, or having a better marriage, or increasing your finances, is one small item. It is a mental photograph in your mind! People create their own monsters and establish their own fears. What picture do you have in your mind that is keeping you from going forward?

Create streams of income to flow into your life in order to improve your financial condition. Creating such streams are not costly at all. You have more ways of producing income at your disposal than you can imagine; you just have to find them. I have 5 different income sources flowing into my life, and I am still searching for new avenues to create more. I intend on developing at least five other streams of income in the next two to five years. As a result of these different income streams, my personal income has risen nearly 200%. As you produce these avenues for income to flow your way, know that when one slows down, the others will most likely continue to feed you. A person once said to me, "You must stay busy?" "Yes.", I replied. If I am not busy then I'm wasting time, and time is of the essence. We are only allotted a certain amount of time on this planet. The unfortunate thing is that we do not know when our time will come to an end. Moreover, since I do not know my time of expiration, I must be diligent about doing what is necessary for my life, my family, and those who I am supposed to help. You have to first make money before you can give money to those in need. Some people are chosen to generate the wealth that blesses many. Your streams of income will keep the cycle of money moving from hand to hand, thus providing income for others as well.

> *You have more ways of producing income at your disposal than you can imagine; you just have to find them.*

Tip #1: Write a book

It costs you nothing but time to sit down and write a book. Everyone has a story in them, and so do you. I have dedicated an entire chapter on the subject of writing and publishing. Read it and it will benefit you as to the many things that can be achieved by becoming an author.

Tip #2   Become a Consultant

Are you good at doing your job? Are you good at any hobby of yours? A consultant is a person who gets paid to give advice to others. This is another way to develop in income that can be rather substantial. You don't have to quit your job to become a paid consultant. You can build a clientele while you are still working at your present job; you must, however, be a skillful manager of time in order to successfully juggle the various demands that will compete for your attention. Depending on your field of expertise, your consulting business can produce as little as $5000 to as much as millions annually. Companies are always looking for consultants who can help their personnel to do a better job.

Tip #3   Start a Staffing Company

I am a consultant to a staffing company that started with less than $100. The company now enjoys contracts in excess of $1.5 million after being in operation for only one year. This company literally started with just a dream and a consultant ... yours truly. I guided the partners through the start-up of their business, and I continue to provide them ongoing advice from time to time. The skills that each of the partners brings to the table is what makes their business operate so well. Charles is very skilled at dealing with the personnel aspects of staffing while Tish is adept at generating new business. They had the knowledge to operate a staffing company, and I simply provided them with the motivation and information on getting started. I simply supplied the mentoring and motivation needed to get their dream from their minds and into the real world. I am reminded of the old Zenith commercials. Their slogan was, "The quality goes in before the name goes on." This slogan was in all of Zenith television commercials and proved to be a successful selling tool for the company. Name recognition is everything. I was instrumental in helping Tish and Charles to develop their company logo that combines parts of their last names. Today "NewTimes Staffing" is a business with strong recognition throughout the business community in our city.

Tip #4   Conduct Your Own Seminars

Here's a wonderful tip.   You don't have to be a seminar speaker to pull it off.   Identify professionals in your community who would like to promote their businesses and you become the broker who put the audience with the professional who wish to speak.   Attorneys, Insurance Salespeople, Real Estate Brokers, and Doctors would love for you to help them to promote their businesses. All you have to do is organize the event, set the fee that attendees will pay, negotiate the speaker's fee, determine seminar expenses, and then walk away with your hefty net profit. You can easily conduct as many as six seminars a year, which will produce a tremendous stream of income. There's a wonderful book on the subject of seminars that I would highly recommend entitled, *"How to Make It BIG in the Seminar Business"* by Paul Karasik. I hope Paul will return the favor and mention my book in his next book. Hey! It's business!

Tip #5   Become a Copywriter

If you are a skilled writer, then you can make good money as a manuscript editor or by creating ideas for commercial advertisers and selling them to television networks or advertising agencies. You'll be surprised by how many small businesses spend countless hours brainstorming ideas for a catchy commercial to advertise their service or product.

You can edit books for a fee. Book editing companies can charge as little as $48 dollars an hour to as much as $160 dollars an hour. If you're good at what you do, then publishing companies will send more business your way.

Tip #6 Start Your Own Photography Business

Many people started with photography as a hobby. You don't have to be all that great; you just have to be good. When I think of national photography companies that recruit young college students who are usually inexperienced but who have been armed with just enough information, I see wasted income potential. The photographers can venture out on their own to do the very thing that the companies pay them to do, but profit greatly in the process. Know that Sears, Walmart, and JC Penny have discovered that big money is in photography. You can run your photography business out of your house; this will greatly reduce expenses. I was able to help a young lady start her own photography business. She already had all the equipment necessary to operate one. She had taken photos before but had never really made any money from it. She and I sat down and brainstormed some ideas and came up with *Yolie's Perfections* Photography. We determined prices, location, and ways to advertise in order to keep business coming in. Never underestimate the importance of a good mentor and coach.

I have assisted many others in starting and growing their businesses - from an accounting business, to a gift-basket business, to restaurant ownership. "Hear the prophet and so shall you prosper" is a paraphrased verse from the bible. The tips stated earlier are only a few of the possible ways of establishing incomes streams for the purpose of helping you to build wealth. These are thought provoking methods that will produce results. And perhaps, one day, you will write about me in one of your books and reveal how some of my suggestions helped you to achieve phenomenal wealth.

Increase Your Income by Becoming an Author

▼

You are an empire of information.
Mikel Brown

CHAPTER 12

Increase Your Income by
Becoming an Author

Okay! You feel as though your life is not interesting enough that others would like to read about your life story. Do you possess information from which others can benefit? Everyone has come through some kind of situation that others may be presently experiencing. Consider writing a book so that you are able to leave a legacy for your children and family members. A book is simply one source that allows individuals to generate wealth by simply putting ideas on paper, but the right book has the potential of bringing financial benefit to your family for generations to come. Dale Carnegie's book entitled, *"How to Win Friends & Influence People"* was first printed in 1936. His children and grandchildren are still benefitting financially from his books to this day. Why write a book? You should author your thoughts because you can and because you have much to say that will be of great benefit to people. Besides, the income potential from the sell of your penned ideas is awesome.

You are a writer, an author, and a publisher just waiting to be exposed. You are an empire of information. There is no better time like the present to begin pitching your information to the world. You possess a wealth of ideas that can greatly revolutionize the way people currently conduct business as well as their personal affairs. Most people hunger for new sources of information, even if some of them may offer redundant information. Inside each of us is a story of love and romance or of pain and disappointment. What causes books to do well in the marketplace is how well they are

> *You possess a wealth of ideas that can greatly revolutionize the way people currently conduct business as well as their personal affairs.*

able to connect with similar experiences that others share. If you are able to offer any useful suggestions to those without answers to their perplexing situations, then you have just found an audience of people waiting for your book to hit store shelves. One author wrote a simple book about his cat and sold thousands of them. How can that be? The success of his book occurred because thousands of cat lovers existed before his book was ever released, but his book simply spoke to the same cat issues that all the others had but chose not to release for the benefit of others. If writing about a family pet is what brought personal satisfaction to the author, then why not make some money in the process.

I can go on and on telling story after story of how ordinary people, just like yourself, wrote books on diverse subject matter from *"The Godfather"* by Mario Puzo to *"Don't Sweat the Small Stuff"* by Richard Carlson. I am sure that you may not want to read about how Greg Godek, author of *"1001 Ways to Be Romantic"* sold over one million books. Do You? Perhaps what you really desire to read about is how he got his book from his computer to the sales counter or off the disk to customers' homes. The reality is that most people never get their book out of the computer. In most cases, they never finished the books they started.

I commend anyone who would undertake the challenging task of writing a book. One of the most exhilarating feelings I have ever experienced in my entire life occurred the first time I received my first book back from the publisher, all shiny and nicely bound. Finishing a book is not half as enjoyable as getting it published and signing your first copy. You will turn somersaults the first time you see your finished work of art sitting on store shelves. Well, you may not be able to pull off doing somersaults, but you will attempt something just as silly.

> *Anybody can write a book, but not just anyone can figure out what to write about.*

Anybody can write a book, but not just anyone can figure out what to write about. People are not generally self-motivated, and it is difficult to get many people to think outside the box. My aim is to convince the housewife, janitor, school teacher, banker, salesperson, minister, mechanic, military person, police officer, dietitian, lawyer, store manager and clerk, and every other person, working or not, that you have a book on the inside of you waiting to be printed on paper and glued to the inside of a soft or hardbound cover. Hollywood is always looking for a good book to turn into a movie, even if it is not a bestseller. Therefore, if you have ever dreamed of writing a book but feel as though your writing skills are not good enough, know that there are ghostwriters whom you can hire for a relatively small fee who can help you get the job done. You really have no excuse. Don't Procrastinate! Start writing your manuscript TODAY!

What do I do after my book is completed?

What a relief! You finally closed out the last chapter of your book. You believe that your book is so good that you will have publishers jumping out of planes and racing their cars to your front door to publish it. Pop open the bubbly, sparkling champagne; it is time to celebrate. Stop and think for a moment. You just finished your book, but no one knows about it but a few of your close friends whom you allowed to read a chapter or two. And because they gave it high praise, you are all ready to get flyers printed for your first book signing. Let's not put the cart before the horse.

Once your book is completed, you must first identify a publisher. You feel confident about your material, but watch out because reality is about to set in. The big question now arises. How do I get my manuscript published? Do I self-publish or do I make my bid for a publisher and have a publishing company do their magic? This can be a tough decision for an author who is unfamiliar with the process of getting a book published. I wish that every first time author was able to avoid those 'I don't know what to do next' blues. The truth is that 98% of all manuscripts written by unknown or first time authors are rejected by traditional publishers. I can hear you saying to yourself, "well, I'll just self-publish my book then." I would not necessarily recommend that you attempt to self-publish because the odds are that you may end up spending anywhere between five hundred to ten thousand dollars. Most authors, without outlets through which to distribute their books, will end up with books piled high in their garage or office. Do not become discourage as a result of what I am sharing with you because I am going to share with you a step-by-step process that will assist you in fulfilling your dreams.

It is necessary to talk about the potential pitfalls involved with any endeavor because you are bound to run into some obstacles along the way. My intentions here are not to mislead you. I simply wish to have you approach the writing and publishing of your book with your eyes wide open. Getting your manuscript published is a labor that is both tedious and yet rewarding. Understand that I am only able to offer the advice that I am providing to you now because I had to learn from the many mistakes I have made along the way in the publication of my several books. As a result of what I have gained over the years, you will be able to greatly minimize the number of mistakes you may make by heeding the suggestions I outline here.

After your book has been completed, your next area of concern is how to market it. Marketing can be more difficult than publishing. Once you have an idea of how you are going to market your book, then you can review the different publishing options. For the sake of answering the question posed as the outset of this chapter, I am going to skip the marketing aspect so that I can put the fire out in your mind regarding what to do now that your book is complete.

What you hope to achieve from the writing of your book is what will help you determine whether it is better to self publish or secure the services of a publisher. If you desire to use your book as a door opener for speaking engagements, I would suggest the self publishing approach because the volume of sales will not be as important to you since your target audience is mainly the people who make the decisions to allow you to speak at their seminars. Self-help books would fall essentially into this category. If on the other hand, your book falls more in the category of fiction, then you would want to lean more in the direction of engaging the help of an established publisher because, in most cases, they will also offer limited promotional assistance to you as part of their fee structure and because you will need to capture the widest audience possible with such books.

If you are going to self publish, I would like to inform you on how the Library of Congress and most book review editors view self-published material. With my first book, it seemed as though I could not buy a written review. When an author self publishes his own material, the publishing industry, book buyers, bookstores, and the media usually frown at their material. I am not suggesting that self published books have never done well; what I am saying is that in order for self published material to do well, there must be a good marketing strategy in place with sufficient moneys to enable the book to penetrate the desired markets. There are a few self-published books that have done well in the marketplace because of the marketing push that the authors were able to apply. Johnson & Blanchard, *The One-Minute Manager* and Eric Weber, *How to Pick up Girls* are among the few self-published

> *Authoring a successful book is 10% writing and 90% marketing.*

authors whose books sold very well. Authoring a successful book is 10% writing and 90% marketing. You will be amazed at the number of doors that will open to you simply because of your status as a published author. Believe it or not, your credibility and marketability escalate exponentially simply by putting your thoughts on paper and selling them.

Self-Help Books Will Sell

People are always looking for books that are motivational and inspiring. Self-help books are categorized in the reference field. Some reference books, unlike novels, are kept around for years in personal and public libraries because they provide information that can be used for many years. Business owners, CEO's, and managers are all in constant pursuit of material that can help them and their employees perform their jobs better.

> *Business owners, CEO's, and managers are all in constant pursuit of material that can help them and their employees perform their jobs better.*

I visited my dentist for a routine procedure and his dental assistant was doing all the preliminary work necessary for the dentist to do his part. While I was waiting for the Dentist to come into the room, the dental assistant started asking questions about my occupation. I informed her that, in addition to my many business pursuits, I am an author and book publisher. She then began to vilify her writing skills and confess that she could never write a book because she had nothing to write about. I responded by asking her, "How well do you know your job?" She replied that she knew her job very because she loved it so much. "There you go." I exclaimed. I went on to say, "You can write a self-help book about how to be a successful dental assistant." "Can you write a book about how a dental assistant can help Dr. Dentist succeed?" I asked. Dentists all over the country would buy this book if you could help their dental assistants to become more proficient at their jobs. Self-help material can be very profitable and personally gratifying because the book also provides a much needed service.

Write about your life, job or your hobbies and watch those profits soar!

"Quotes" for Success

CHAPTER 4
*"The road to wealth should be a well-planned,
methodical journey."*

CHAPTER 5
"Your challenge will appear when your prior knowledge begins
to clash with your new knowledge."

CHAPTER 6
"No danger can arise in rooting out bad principles."

CHAPTER 9
"The rich see opportunities to work and
invest their money, and in their ideas"

CHAPTER 10
"It is not the material of the dream that matters;
it is what the dream does that you commit to."

CHAPTER 11
"You don't have to know how to do a thing well;
you just have to know what to do."

CHAPTER 12
"You are an empire of information."

Notes

Notes

Notes

Power Communications Network

Empowering A Generation Through Communications

Mikel Brown, CEO

"Life-changing" is the word to describe Mikel Brown's ability to articulate a message that is able to permeate the soul of a person. He is a well-traveled businessman, lecturer and author whose appeal is from selling to religion.

Mikel Brown's clients have included:

*K-Mart,
*Evangelical Christian Leaders
*and several Universities

For speaking engagements, seminars, conventions, business meetings, salesmen conclave, employee motivational work shops, or church conventions,

**Please contact;
Pat Cruz
1-915-595-1307
or
www.buildinguwealth.com**

Printed in the United States
22116LVS00002B/79-159